UNDER THE MANAGEMENT OF
MR. CHARLES DICKENS

His Production of "The Frozen Deep"

Frontispiece: Private Theatricals at Tavistock House—Scene from "The Frozen Deep," Act III

The cave mouth is the Tavistock House schoolroom bay, from which the windows were removed. The seascape with its ship flying the British ensign was painted by Clarkson Stanfield, R.A., and hung in a thirty-foot room that Dickens designed and had built in his garden especially for the performance. Richard Wardour (Dickens) lies in the foreground, making his dying revelations to Lt. Crayford (Mark Lemon). Clara Burnham (Mary Dickens) kneels with her back to the audience, hiding Frank Aldersley (Wilkie Collins). Lucy Crayford (Georgina Hogarth) looks askance at Wardour. Mrs. Steventon (Ellen Hogarth) stands beside her. The bearded man is Captain Ebsworth (Edward Pigott); the young man beside him is Lt. Steventon (Charles Dickens, Jr.). The remaining woman, her face turned from the audience, is Rose Ebsworth (Kate Dickens). (From *The Illustrated London News,* XXX, No. 840 [January 17, 1857], 51.)

UNDER ♣ ♣ ♣ ♣ ♣ ♣
THE MANAGEMENT OF
MR. CHARLES DICKENS

HIS PRODUCTION OF "The Frozen Deep"

Edited by ROBERT LOUIS BRANNAN

Hiram College

CORNELL UNIVERSITY PRESS—*Ithaca, New York*

PR4494
.F7
1966

CORNELL UNIVERSITY PRESS
First published 1966

Library of Congress Catalog Card Number: 66–22927
PRINTED IN THE UNITED STATES OF AMERICA
BY KINGSPORT PRESS, INC.

To my wife

Acknowledgments

This edition of the script for the 1857 production of "The Frozen Deep" has been made possible through the assistance of many persons. My primary obligations are to the Pierpont Morgan Library and Mr. Frederick B. Adams, Jr., its Director, and to Mr. Henry Charles Dickens, Dickens' heir, who have given permission for the manuscripts to be edited and published. I am indebted also to Mr. Herbert Cahoon, Curator of Autograph Manuscripts at the Pierpont Morgan Library, and his staff, who assisted me in reading obscure passages of the manuscripts. Miss D. L. Minards and Mrs. Madeline House helped to identify the authors of articles in *Household Words*. Mr. Leslie C. Staples, editor of *The Dickensian,* has answered several queries. I have found K. J. Fielding's comments on the Collins-Dickens relationship, George Ford's history of the Victorian audience, Humphry House's explanation of Dickens' humanism, and Edmund Wilson's analysis of Dickens' psychology particularly useful; Walter Dexter's edition of the letters in *The Nonesuch Dickens* and Edgar Johnson's biography and edition of Dickens' letters to Miss Coutts were invaluable. I am grateful to the Danforth Foundation and to the University of Notre Dame for grants which freed me for a year of research. Finally, I wish to thank all my professors at Cornell, who have encouraged and assisted my work in many ways. I owe a heavy debt to those who read the manuscript and offered suggestions about its content or style—Professors Robert Donovan, James McConkey, and especially Francis Mineka and Taylor Stoehr.

R. L. B.

South Bend, Indiana
February 1966

Contents

Illustrations

UNDER THE MANAGEMENT OF
MR. CHARLES DICKENS

His Production of "The Frozen Deep"

Introduction

In January of 1857 select audiences, including the Chief Justices of England, the President of the Royal Academy, and professional reviewers, watched an amateur cast perform in a romantic drama, "The Frozen Deep," billed as by Wilkie Collins. The audiences came expecting an amusing evening, for the manager and star performer was Charles Dickens. Indeed Dickens was also a principal author of the script. He had established a reputation as an unusually competent manager of amateur productions, but the quality and effect of these performances of "The Frozen Deep" surprised even his staunchest admirers. Dickens' acting in the death scene drew tears from men and women alike. The reviewers judged the performances to be superior to anything on the professional stage; some thought the acting, especially Dickens', so unusual that its example might revolutionize the professional theater. The unexpected success of the first performances on the Tavistock House stage led to performances in July and August before Queen Victoria and thousands of ordinary theatergoers. Dickens affected his later audiences as powerfully as he had the guests in his home; members of the Royal Party and experienced stage carpenters wept as they watched Dickens portray the death of Richard Wardour. Reviewers, surveying the series of performances, hailed them as the outstanding dramatic event of 1857.

The play was again staged in 1866, at the Royal Olympic

Theatre—this time with a professional manager and a professional cast. Wilkie Collins had revised the 1857 script and had printed, but not published, copies of the altered script for the professional cast to use.[1] But the presumably improved 1866 production was jeered by the audiences and failed even to pay expenses. Discouraged by the failure, Collins did nothing further with the dramatic version and refused numerous requests from amateur groups for permission to produce it.[2] For his last public reading in America in 1874, he rewrote the 1866 dramatic version as a narrative, which was then published in *Temple Bar* and in a collection of stories.[3] This is the only published, and the only readily accessible, version of "The Frozen Deep." In the introduction to the collection, Collins remarks that the narrative closely follows Acts II and III of the play. By "the play" he must have meant the 1866 version, for the narrative differs greatly from the script that Dickens used in the 1857 performances.

Neither of the dramatic versions is a good play. The 1857 script has some permanent importance, however, because that version attained a striking success, and because Dickens helped

[1] Wilkie Collins, "The Frozen Deep: A Drama in Three Acts" (printed in London, 1866; copy used, Acc. No. 43002, Pierpont Morgan Library). Leslie C. Staples, editor of *The Dickensian*, owns Collins' personal copy of this printing; on the wrapper appears in Collins' hand, "Reconsidered Corrections (copy these in case of necessity) W.C." For the practice of printing, but not publishing, see Allardyce Nicoll, *A History of English Drama, 1660–1900* (6 vols.; Cambridge, Eng., 1959), V, 231.

[2] Wilkie Collins to Mr. Kent, February 3, 1881, *The Dickensian*, V (1909), 161.

[3] Wilkie Collins, "The Frozen Deep: A Dramatic Story in Five Scenes," *Temple Bar*, XLII (1874), 1–21, 145–164, 289–316, and *The Frozen Deep and Other Stories* (2 vols.; London, 1874), I, 2–220.

to write it, controlled every detail of its staging, and acted the principal role. In particular, Dickens appears to have suggested the original idea for the play and, beginning in August 1856, to have given it all the time he could spare from *Little Dorrit* and *Household Words*. He worked closely with Collins on the script, made expensive modifications of Tavistock House, supervised gas fitters and scene painters, selected and trained the amateur cast. He climaxed his activities by appearing as "what was and is in fact the one character in the play, the part written for Mr. Dickens, Richard Wardour." [4] He acted this role with such intensity that, after the performances, he often found himself near collapse. In his appearances as Wardour, he found relief from the marital unhappiness and well-known unrest that agitated him during 1856 and 1857. Months after the last performance, he continued to refer to this relief.

The text for the 1857 script has existed in a manuscript labeled by Dickens as "The Prompt-Book." [5] In October 1856, Collins had given the first draft of the script to Dickens, who then revised it. From this revised draft, Dickens, Charles, Jr., and Mark Lemon made the fair copy, the prompt-book, used for the 1857 performances. Members of the cast copied their parts from it. After rehearsals began, Dickens revised the script still further. He apparently kept the prompt-book until 1860, when he gave it to Collins, who until then had had only a rough draft. [6]

[4] *The Examiner*, November 10, 1866, p. 711.

[5] This prompt-book manuscript, the revised draft from which it was copied, and several letters relating to "The Frozen Deep," some unpublished, are owned by the Pierpont Morgan Library, which identifies the collection as M.A. 81.

[6] Dickens to Collins, June 2, 1860: "I think you said you had found a rough copy of the Frozen Deep. Nevertheless in sending you home Antonina I think it wise to send you the Promptbook" (M.A. 81).

Collins used the prompt-book as a working draft in 1866, altering it extensively in preparing the script printed for the professional cast. The 1857 script has never before been printed.

The prompt-book manuscript consists of sixty-nine large quarto leaves, many written on both sides. Roughly forty pages of stage directions, instructions for the prompter, and dialogue are in Dickens' handwriting. The 1866 alterations have obscured and even obliterated parts of the earlier script. Collins deleted portions of the original and made additions between the lines or on the backs of leaves, some of which also contain stage directions and dialogue previously added in Dickens' handwriting. Fortunately, in making these alterations Collins used a much darker ink than was used by Dickens, Charles, Jr., and Lemon in making the 1857 fair copy and by Dickens in making his revisions. By a comparison of this manuscript with the 1866 printed text and the revised draft from which the fair copy was made, Collins' alterations can be identified and the 1857 reading determined, even in those passages obscured by his deletions. The editing principles will be explained in the "Note on the Text of the Play"; the general intent of the present edition has been to recover the final script used by Dickens.

Even when the text of this script has been established, it still presents a problem, because it is little more than the skeleton of an unconventional melodrama. It makes the intense excitement of Dickens and the enthusiastic praise of admirers, including professional reviewers, W. C. Macready, and Queen Victoria, seem incomprehensible. But the script is skeletal because it is little more than a scenario. From the beginning, "The Frozen Deep" was planned as a peculiar kind of stage performance with the script to be merely an essential means for implementing this performance. The performance, not the script, excited Dickens and his audiences. All the reviewers knew that it was Dickens' synthesis of the various elements of the stage performance which made it seem so strikingly harmonious, novel, and powerful. Two important reviewers judged that Dickens, in the part of Wardour, had transcended the limits of the script's character sketch; he had moved his audiences more intensely than the dialogue or situations could account for.

Dickens was able to achieve this kind of performance because his conception of the play was partly independent of Collins' script. This conception apparently grew from Dickens' dissatisfaction with his personal life, his irritation with the canons of respectability that restricted his artistic imagination, and his interest in defending a faith in man. When Collins wrote the script, he tailored it to meet the requirements of a notion suggested by Dickens and of an amateur cast selected by Dickens. Finding that the script did not meet these requirements, Dickens extensively revised it. Dickens' part in the genesis of the idea and of the script and Dickens' contributions as manager and actor make the 1857 version of "The Frozen Deep" at least as much Dickens' work as Collins'. In any event, the importance of the play arises not from the negligible artistic merits of the script, but from the contributions of Dickens to the play as theater and from the impact of the stage performance on Dickens and his audience.

Genesis

Dickens' interest in amateur theatricals may encourage the reader to regard "The Frozen Deep" as merely another Tavistock House production, and consequently to ignore or neglect its peculiarities and Dickens' distinctive contributions. After buying Tavistock House in 1851, Dickens produced a minor drama on each Twelfth Night to amuse his children and a few friends. In the summer of 1855, he even produced an adult theatrical, Wilkie Collins' "The Lighthouse." Collins, whose last novel had not sold well, had been thinking of a career as a playwright and had asked Dickens to advise him about the script. As a "little lark," Dickens himself had decided to produce the "regular old-style melodrama." [7] It is easy to assume that "The Frozen Deep" was merely another old-style melodrama, and that in producing it Dickens engaged in a familiar activity, intensified only because his emotional unrest drove him to seek an escape from his ordinary activities. Neither Dickens nor his contemporaries, however, viewed "The Frozen Deep" as being like the plays which had preceded it. After surveying the series of Tavistock House theatricals, Charles, Jr., remarked, "On the sixth of January, 1857, the Tavistock House theatricals reached their climax in the production of Wilkie Collins's 'Frozen Deep.' This was a very ambitious effort indeed, as far beyond the 'Lighthouse' as the 'Lighthouse' was in advance of 'Guy Fawkes' and 'William Tell.' " [8] Charles, Jr., probably knew little about the genesis of

[7] Dickens to Clarkson Stanfield, May 20, 1855, in *The Letters of Charles Dickens,* ed. Walter Dexter (3 vols.; Bloomsbury, 1938), II, 663 (these volumes of *The Nonesuch Dickens* will hereafter be referred to as *Letters*).

[8] Charles Dickens, Jr., "Reminiscences of My Father," *The Windsor Magazine,* supp. (December 1934), p. 20.

TAVISTOCK HOUSE THEATRE.

UNDER THE MANAGEMENT OF, MR. CHARLES DICKENS.

On *Twelfth Night, Tuesday, January 6th,* 1857, AT A QUARTER BEFORE 8 O'CLOCK, *will be presented*

AN ENTIRELY NEW

ROMANTIC DRAMA, IN THREE ACTS, BY MR. WILKIE COLLINS,

CALLED

THE FROZEN DEEP.

The Machinery and Properties by MR. IRELAND, *of the Theatre Royal, Adelphi.* *The Dresses by* MESSRS. NATHAN, *of Titchbourne Street, Haymarket. Perruquier,* MR. WILSON, *of the Strand.*

THE PROLOGUE WILL BE DELIVERED BY MR. JOHN FORSTER.

CAPTAIN EBSWORTH, *of The Sea Mew*	MR. EDWARD PIGOTT.
CAPTAIN HELDING, *of The Wanderer*	MR. ALFRED DICKENS.
LIEUTENANT CRAYFORD	MR. MARK LEMON.
FRANK ALDERSLEY	MR. WILKIE COLLINS.
RICHARD WARDOUR	MR. CHARLES DICKENS.
LIEUTENANT STEVENTON	MR. YOUNG CHARLES.
JOHN WANT, *Ship's Cook*	MR. AUGUSTUS EGG, A.R.A.
BATESON } *Two of The Sea Mew's People*	{ MR. EDWARD HOGARTH.
DARKER }	{ MR. FREDERICK EVANS.

(OFFICERS AND CREWS OF THE SEA MEW AND WANDERER.)

MRS. STEVENTON	MISS HELEN.
ROSE EBSWORTH	MISS KATE.
LUCY CRAYFORD	MISS HOGARTH.
CLARA BURNHAM	MISS MARY.
NURSE ESTHER	MRS. WILLS.
MAID	MISS MARTHA.

THE SCENERY AND SCENIC EFFECTS OF THE FIRST ACT, BY MR. TELBIN.
THE SCENERY AND SCENIC EFFECTS OF THE SECOND AND THIRD ACTS, BY Mr. STANFIELD, R.A.
ASSISTED BY MR. DANSON.
THE ACT-DROP, ALSO BY Mr. STANFIELD, R.A.

AT THE END OF THE PLAY, HALF-AN-HOUR FOR REFRESHMENT.

To Conclude with MRS. INCHBALD's Farce, in Two Acts, of

ANIMAL MAGNETISM.

(THE SCENE IS LAID IN SEVILLE.)

THE DOCTOR	MR. CHARLES DICKENS.
PEDRILLO	MR. MARK LEMON.
THE MARQUIS DE LA GUARDIA	MR. YOUNG CHARLES.
GREGORIO	MR. WILKIE COLLINS.
CAMILLA	MISS KATE.
JACINTHA	MISS HOGARTH.

Musical Composer and Conductor of the Orchestra—Mr. FRANCESCO BERGER, who will preside at the Piano.

CARRIAGES MAY BE ORDERED AT HALF-PAST ELEVEN.

GOD SAVE THE QUEEN!

Playbill for the Opening Performance at Tavistock House,
January 6, 1857

A dress rehearsal, attended by the servants and a few friends, was held on January 5. (From Part III, *Charles Dickens Rare Print Collection,* ed. Seymour Eaton [printed for private circulation; Philadelphia, 1900]; reproduced by permission of Cornell University.)

the play, but having acted in it, he remained vividly aware that the performances had excited his father and the audiences extraordinarily. He was aware, also, that unlike any other play produced at Tavistock House, "The Frozen Deep" had been tailored for Dickens and his amateur cast. In producing other theatricals, Dickens had modified scripts freely, but he had not had a script specifically written for him.[9] Dickens' contributions to this script and his success in the stage performances distinguish "The Frozen Deep" significantly from any other play that drew his interest.

In 1856 personal problems apparently caused Dickens to long for the escape that producing a play could offer, and they undoubtedly heightened his interest in "The Frozen Deep." About the time that he conceived the idea for the play, Dickens wrote to John Forster:

I have always felt of myself that I must, please God, die in harness, but I have never felt it more strongly than in looking at, and thinking of, him [W. C. Macready]. However strange it is to be never at rest, and never satisfied, and ever trying after something that is never reached, and to be always laden with plot and plan and care and worry, how clear it is that it must be, and that one is driven by an irresistible might until the journey is worked out! It is much better to go on and fret, than to stop and fret. As to repose—for some men there's no such thing in this life. The foregoing has the appearance of a small sermon; but it is so often in my head in these

---

[9] In 1851, Edward Bulwer-Lytton had written an episodic comedy, *Not So Bad As We Seem,* for Dickens and a group of prominent amateurs. In a sense, this was "tailored" for Dickens and an amateur cast (see Ernest Bliss Finch, "The Mid-Victorian Theatre as Seen by Its Critics: 1850–1870" [unpublished Ph.D. dissertation, Cornell University, 1951], pp. 141–142).

days that it cannot help coming out. . . . I find that the skeleton in my domestic closet is becoming a pretty big one.[10]

W. C. Macready had apparently aged rapidly after his retirement from the stage in 1851 and had found restless discontent rather than repose. Disturbed by the change in Macready, Dickens reflected on his own discontent. His marriage was becoming increasingly painful. Partly, perhaps largely, because of this pain, he gained little satisfaction from his normal work and found no hope of permanent relief except in death. He found temporary relief only in his work, which, though it brought no great peace, made his life meaningful. He was convinced that he would be able to continue this work because he was impelled by an "irresistible might," presumably some force in his own nature, which would prevent his ever imitating Macready. Despite his conviction, however, Dickens called his reflections a "small sermon," implying that he recognized as a temptation the possibility of throwing off the "harness." The skeleton in his domestic closet was growing and his life's journey under the burden of emotional stress could become unendurable. He was sustained by his faith in the power of the "irresistible might" rather than by hope that his burden would lessen. His faith in the possibility of endurance, his concept of life as a difficult journey, and his belief that final repose could be found only in death are all important elements in the development of Richard Wardour.

"The Frozen Deep" undoubtedly is associated with moods like the ones stimulated by Macready. Performing as Richard Wardour, Dickens found his faith in the "irresistible might" strengthened. In several letters to Collins, to John Foster, and to Mrs. Richard Watson, Dickens commented freely on his relief

[10] April 1856, *Letters*, II, 765.

during the performances and on his intensified unrest as soon as these had ended. Seven months after the last performance, Dickens wrote to Collins, "The domestic unhappiness remains so strong upon me that I can't write, and (waking) can't rest, one minute. I have never known a moment's peace or content, since the last night of the Frozen Deep." [11] Within two years, the emotional stress had become so severe that Dickens could no longer continue his daily work, much less the long and difficult journey. What had caused him to fret, now threatened to destroy him. When one knows Dickens' part in the genesis of the play, his remarks to Forster and to Collins may suggest that Wardour's role provided Dickens with a specific kind of relief rather than with the mere escape that he might have found in any amateur theatrical.

Dickens' unrest in 1856 was heightened by his growing desire to create a new kind of hero and by his fear that he was alienated from a substantial portion of his readers. He felt that the moralistic expectations of these readers imposed limits on his artistic imagination. These limits exasperated him. About them, Dickens wrote to Forster:

I have always a fine feeling of the honest state into which we have got, when some smooth gentleman says to me . . . how odd it is that the hero of an English book is always uninteresting—too good—not natural. . . . But O my smooth friend, what a shining imposter you must think yourself and what an ass you must think me, when you suppose that by putting a brazen face upon it you can blot out of my knowledge the fact that this same unnatural young gentleman

[11] March 21, 1858, *Letters*, III, 14. See also Dickens to Collins, August 29, 1857, *Letters*, II, 873; to John Forster, September 5, 1857, September [n.d.], 1857, October 1857, *Letters*, II, 877–878, 887–888; to Mrs. Richard Watson, December 7, 1857, *The Dickensian*, XXXVIII (1942), 189–191.

(if to be decent is to be necessarily unnatural), whom you meet in
those other books and in mine, *must be* presented to you in that
unnatural aspect by reason of your morality, and is not to have, I will
not say any of the indecencies you like, but not even any of the
experiences, trials, perplexities, and confusions inseparable from the
making or unmaking of all men! [12]

Dickens admitted the charge that his own heroes were unnatu-
rally good, in the sense of lacking serious inner conflicts or
confusions. In making this admission and blaming the hypocritical morality of respectability, Dickens implied that he wanted
to create a hero who would be more natural or realistic than the
ones in his own novels. He was not interested in the superficial
sensationalism that might be achieved by dramatizing indecent
behavior. He was interested in a fully mature man. Dickens
believed that inner trials were "inseparable from the making or
unmaking of all men." Without dramatizing some inner struggle, the creative artist could not present a fully developed man,
much less a hero. Being made a "man" would mean enduring
severe inner trials and remaining faithful to a personal ideal of
conduct. The hero's personality and character, not his reputation, would be at stake during the trials. Being unmade would
mean weakening under stress and committing some action so
heinous that the personality and character would be destroyed.
The group of middle-class readers, however, on whom all popular novelists depended for their sales, included many women
who might be unfamiliar with, and offended by, such struggles.
It also included men who might pretend to be unfamiliar with,
and offended by, them; such "smooth gentlemen" infuriated
Dickens. The ethic of respectability seemed to taboo the inner
struggles necessary to reveal a man's real stature. Dickens feared

[12] August 15, 1856, *Letters*, II, 797.

that violating such a taboo would decrease the sales of his novels, and he resented the restrictive force the fear imposed on his creative imagination. The private theatricals at Tavistock House afforded Dickens an opportunity to escape this restriction.

Accounts of early nineteenth-century British expeditions searching for a Northwest Passage in the Arctic regions provided material from which such a hero could be drawn. "The Frozen Deep" takes its most important symbol and the setting for its most important scenes from these Arctic expeditions. One of the best known was that of Sir John Franklin, who, eventually, was credited with having discovered the Passage. Franklin, a popular hero, had disappeared while commanding an Arctic exploration. Charges of cannibalism had been brought against his expedition, implicitly against him, in 1854. These charges caused a public controversy, temporarily stilled by concern about the Crimean War. At the time the play was being planned and performed, this controversy had been renewed by demands that the government finance another search to find evidence with which the charges could be refuted.

From 1854 to 1857, Dickens printed in *Household Words* seven articles defending Franklin and encouraging another expedition. In November 1854 and again in March or April 1856, Dickens was in contact with Lady Franklin, the wife of the explorer, who was stirring the public demands for the search and offering her personal fortune to support it. Finally, in May 1857, Dickens appeared as the representative of periodical literature and the press at a dinner given by the Royal Geographical Society to wish "success to the projected final search for Sir John Franklin" and the "health of the explorers of distant regions." [13] To understand both Dickens' contributions to the play and the

[13] *The Times*, May 26, 1857, p. 12.

audience's reaction to it, one has to know something about Sir John Franklin, the charges against him, and Dickens' defense. In 1818, Franklin, who had fought at Trafalgar with Nelson, commanded a ship in an expedition searching for the Northwest Passage. From 1819 to 1821, he had commanded his own expedition, exploring the area to the east of Hudson Bay. In 1825, he left his dying wife, at her own urging, in a third futile attempt to find the Passage. He returned to England in 1827, remarried in 1828, and was knighted in 1829. After serving as Governor of Van Diemen's Land for several years, he began planning his final expedition in 1843. On May 19, 1845, the fifty-nine-year-old Franklin sailed in command of this expedition, consisting of 129 men and officers equipped with supplies for three years. The expedition was last seen on July 26, 1845. About the time in 1848 that the supplies would have been exhausted, search expeditions were formed, eventually involving hundreds of men and dozens of ships, including two from America. The British government offered a reward of £10,000 for either the rescue of the expedition or the discovery of its fate.

This reward was claimed by Dr. John Rae, Chief Factor of the Hudson's Bay Company. While exploring the region north of Repulse Bay in April 1854, Rae met a group of Eskimos who had heard that a party of white men had died a great distance to the west. Investigating, he found other Eskimos who possessed articles bearing Franklin's crest and who claimed to have obtained the articles from another group of Eskimos who had seen the bodies of thirty-five to forty white men. These bodies were reported to have been mutilated and the cooking pots near them to have contained human flesh. After a brief, unsuccessful search for this last group of Eskimos and for the bodies, Rae sailed for England. Relying on the hearsay evidence and the Franklin relics, which he had purchased, he announced to the public that the Franklin expedition had met a fate "as terrible as the imagination can conceive." He asserted, unequivocally, that "our wretched countrymen had been driven to the last resource —cannibalism—as a means of prolonging existence." [14] The assertion created a general stir and greatly disturbed part of the public. *The Times* refused to accept his report as final. An editorial writer argued that if Eskimos could live through "starving times," it would be "strange indeed that the white men should not have been able to accomplish the same feat." He urged that steps be taken as soon as possible "for solving one of the most painful problems of our times." [15] Hendrik van Loon remarks that as long as his father lived, his father remembered the "shock of horror that had swept across the civilized world" as the news of Rae's report spread. [16]

Dickens may not have read the report when it was first printed, for on November 20, he wrote to W. H. Wills:

It has occurred to me that I am rather strong on Voyages and Cannibalism, and might do an interesting little paper for the next No. on that part of Dr. Rae's report, taking the arguments against its probabilities. Can you get me a newspaper cutting containing his report? If not, will you have it copied for me and sent up to Tavistock House straight way. [17]

The "interesting little paper" was printed as two *Household Words* lead articles. Dickens apparently was agitated after he read the report and judged that the evidence was weak for the kind of conclusion Rae had drawn from it. He thought that Rae

[14] *The Times,* October 23, 1854, p. 7. For a full report see *Further Papers Relative to the Recent Arctic Expeditions in Search of Sir John Franklin and the Crews of H. M. S. "Erebus" and "Terror"* (London, 1855), pp. 331 ff.
[15] October 26, 1854, p. 6.
[16] *Van Loon's Lives* (New York, 1942), pp. 817–818.
[17] November 20, 1854, *Letters,* II, 606.

might have made a more careful investigation before hurrying back to England and that he might have been more hesitant about accepting hearsay testimony from Eskimo witnesses, who, in Dickens' opinion, were "covetous, treacherous, and cruel" savages. Expressing concern for "those who take the nearest and dearest interest in the fate of that unfortunate expedition," Dickens became Franklin's public defender.

Dickens based his defense on two grounds—the character of the Eskimo witnesses and the character of Franklin himself. Dickens attacked the credibility of the Eskimos in general, saying that savages were natural liars, but spent much of his scorn on Rae's interpreter:

Ninety-nine interpreters out of a hundred, whether savage, half-savage, or wholly civilized, interpreting to a person of superior station and attainments, will be under a strong temptation to exaggerate. This temptation will always be strongest precisely where the person interpreted to is seen to be the most excited and impressed by what he hears; for in proportion as he is moved, the interpreter's importance is increased.[18]

This attack on the Eskimos was only incidental to the second defense, which Dickens called "analogy." He argued that because Franklin had resisted terrible stresses on previous expeditions, Franklin had proved himself a type of hero for whom cannibalism would have been virtually a moral impossibility. When Franklin and his men previously had descended "far into the valley of the shadow of Death," they had lain "down side by side, calmly and even cheerfully awaiting their release from this world."[19] Franklin, as commander of the expedition, had played a special role, "infusing into it, as such a man necessarily must,

[18] "The Lost Arctic Voyagers," *Household Words*, December 2, 1854, pp. 361–362.
[19] Page 362.

the force of his character and discipline, patience and fortitude." [20] Dickens concluded his defense in the first article thus:

Heaven forbid that we, sheltered and fed, and considering this
question at our warm hearth, should audaciously set limits to any
extremity of desperate distress! It is in reverence for the brave and
enterprising, in admiration for the great spirits who can endure even
unto the end, in love for their names, and in tenderness for their
memory, that we think of the specks, once ardent men, "scattered
about in different positions" on the waste of ice and snow, and plead
for their lightest ashes . . . as the citadel of the position, that the
better educated the man, the better disciplined the habits, the more
reflective and religious the tone of thought, the more gigantically
improbable the "last resource" becomes.[21]

The defense on the ground of "analogy" ended as an appeal to
the faith in the British gentleman and hero.

The second article, devoted entirely to distinguishing the British hero from ordinary men, continued this appeal.[22] Dickens
cited several instances of cannibalism, chiefly among foreign
seamen. In part, his citations attempt to show that the men who
resorted to the "last resource" were in more desperate situations
than Franklin's men. Dickens' comments, however, emphasize
two points, that such men were degraded before they were placed
under stress, and that while under stress the men lacked the
support of such heroic commanders as Bligh and Franklin. Dickens ended his long series of citations with a homily:

In weighing the probabilities and improbabilities of the "last resource," the foremost question is—not the nature of the extremity;
but, the nature of the men. We submit that the memory of the lost

[20] "The Lost Arctic Voyagers," December 2, p. 363.
[21] Page 365.
[22] "The Lost Arctic Voyagers," *Household Words*, December 9, 1854,
pp. 385–393.

Arctic voyagers is placed, by reason and experience, high above the taint of this so easily-allowed connection; and that the noble conduct and example of such men, and of their great leader himself, under similar endurances, belies it, and outweighs by the weight of the whole universe the chatter of a gross handful of uncivilized people, with a domesticity of blood and blubber. Utilitarianism will protest "they are dead; why care about this?" Our reply shall be, "Because they ARE dead, therefore we care about this. Because they served their country well, and deserved well of her, and can ask, no more on this earth, for her justice or her loving-kindness; give them both, full measure, pressed down, running over. Because no Franklin can come back, to write the honest story of their woes and resignation, read it tenderly and truly in the book he has left us. Because they lie scattered on those wastes of snow . . . therefore, cherish them gently, even in the breasts of children. Therefore, teach no one to shudder without reason, at the history of their end. Therefore, confide with their own firmness, in their fortitude, their lofty sense of duty, their courage, and their religion.[23]

The testimony on which Dickens relied most heavily was provided by the previous experience of the explorers themselves as revealed in "the book" that Franklin had left. This book was Franklin's journal, containing a few sections written by Dr. John Richardson, Franklin's Arctic companion and friend.[24] For Dickens, the principal interest of the journal lay not in the new geographical discoveries, but in the reaction of the men to forces of nature that dwarfed and threatened to destroy them. In the journal, the sketches drawn by Lt. George Back, R.N., a member of the expedition, emphasize these forces; tiny human figures are overshadowed by gigantic mountains and glaciers. In the accompanying narrative, Franklin indicated that the men

[23] "The Lost Arctic Voyagers," December 9, pp. 392–393.
[24] John Franklin, *Narrative of a Journey to the Shores of the Polar Sea, in the Years 1819, 20, 21* (London, 1823).

were often threatened not only by physical extinction, but also by moral extinction, with being "unmade" in Dickens' sense of that term. Writing of a time when the men had been driven, under the stress of hunger, to eat weeds, the contents of a deer's stomach, and raw intestines, Franklin remarked that "every tender feeling was suspended by the desire for self-preservation." [25] And referring to an attempted desertion, he wrote, "It is painful to have to record a fact so derogatory to human nature, but I have deemed it proper to mention it, to shew the difficulties we had to contend with, and the effect which distress had in warping the feelings and understanding of the most diligent and obedient of our party." [26] The main point of such remarks was to emphasize that although human nature was warped by distress, it did not break, especially in the leaders. The suspension of the tender feelings was important because the consequence was a confused understanding. Had the deserter succeeded in escaping, he would have committed an irrevocable action by the standards of the British naval tradition, marking himself for life as an outlaw. Further, the desertion would have encouraged panic among the others at a time when the only hope for survival lay in every man's doing his duty. This was why the "fact" was "so derogatory to human nature." Franklin did not apologize for the indecorous behaviour of the men in eating the raw intestines. The "smooth gentleman" might have found this more offensive than the attempted desertion.

When Dickens asserted that the foremost question was not the nature of the extremity, but the nature of the men, he referred to men who had proved their courage, compassion, and fidelity under conditions of terrible stress. He identified the general enemy of such men as "Utilitarianism," but apparently he used this term very loosely. The real enemy seems to have

[25] *Narrative*, p. 441.   [26] *Narrative*, p. 442.

Preparing an Encampment of the Barren Grounds: Gathering Tripe de Roche &c Sept' 16

This and the other illustrations in Franklin's *Journal* were originally prepared from drawings brought back to England by Lt. George Back, a member of the expedition. *Tripe de roche* was the name applied by the explorers to the various types of lichens with which they supplemented their diet when game was scarce. (From John Franklin's *Narrative of a Journey to the Shores of the Polar Sea in the Years 1819, 20, 21, and 22* [London, 1828]; reproduced by permission of Cornell University.)

Dram: Pers:

Captain Ebsworth, of the Sea Mew	7 Pigott.
Captain Helding, of the Wanderer	alfred Dickens
Lieutenant Crayford	mark Lemon.
Frank Aldersley	Wilkie Collins
Richard Wardour	Charles Dickens
Lieutenant Steventon	Charley.
John Want	Augustus Egg.
Bateson } Two of the Sea Mew's people	Edward Hogarth
Parker }	Frederick Evans
Officers and Sailors	

Mrs Steventon	Ellen Hogarth
Rose Ebsworth	Katie
Lucy Crayford	Georgina
Clara Burnham	Mary
Nurse Esther	Mrs Wills
Maid.	

The Prompt-Book—Dramatis Personnae

This whole page is in Dickens' handwriting, but there is no way of determining who deleted the actors' names. Characteristic of Dickens' hand are the peculiar capitals of "Pers:," "Pigott," "Bateson," and "Georgina," the *y* in "Crayford," and the g in "Georgina." Note, however, that the *y* at the end of "Charley" and the g in "Pigott" are also Dickens'. (From M.A. 81, Pierpont Morgan Library; reproduced by permission of the Trustees of the Library.)

been excessive rationalism, egoism, Pharisaism—any belief that belittled or devalued the sentiments on which heroic endurance depended. Dickens regarded such sentiments as essential attributes of human nature. In defending Franklin, Dickens defended his own faith in man's power to endure under stress, and the source of this power lay not so much in man's reason and will as in man's heart. The absence of courage, hope, compassion, or fidelity would make heroic endurance and purposeful action impossible. Because Dickens viewed these primarily as sentiments rather than as consciously acquired virtues, the threat was always present for him that an absence of feeling could forebode a man's being "unmade." The frozen Arctic wastes were demonstrably a force that could cause the suspension of noble sentiments. Franklin was a witness to the faith, however, that a heroic man possessed a heart resistant to the pressure of such a force.

Rae replied to Dickens in a long detailed report, which Dickens printed in two parts.[27] Appealing to his own experience, Rae defended the character of the Eskimos and of his interpreter, restated his reasons for hurrying back to England, and asserted that members of the Arctic expeditions had characters less noble than Dickens attributed to them. With Rae's reply, Dickens reprinted a short section from Franklin's journal which confirmed his judgment of the Eskimos. Then, a month later, he reprinted Rae's original report with a brief comment about its being "a very unsatisfactory document" on which to found the kind of conclusions that Rae had drawn. The comment concluded, "The preoccupation of the public mind has dismissed the subject easily for the present; but, we assume its great

[27] "The Lost Arctic Voyagers," *Household Words,* December 23, 1854, pp. 433–437, and "Dr. Rae's Report," *Household Words,* December 30, 1854, pp. 457–459.

interest, and the serious doubts we hold of its having been convincingly set at rest, to be absolutely certain to revive." [28] The pressing issues of the Crimean War made it difficult to stir strong public feeling over the issue of justice to the memory of men apparently dead, and awkward to urge that the government continue expensive searches on the chance of finding survivors or facts with which to confute Rae. Dickens could do nothing more, at the time, in defense of Franklin's memory and the faith in the nature of men symbolized for him by that memory.

As Dickens had predicted, interest revived early in 1856 after the end of the Crimean War. Lady Franklin inspired much of the interest by appeals to the Lords of the Admiralty for a new search expedition. [29] Dickens had sent copies of his 1854 articles to Lady Franklin. [30] In March or April 1856, when she was beginning her appeals, she sent him a copy of an Arctic memoir which he apparently had not read previously. "Lady Franklin sent me the whole of that Richardson memoir; and I think Richardson's manly friendship, and love of Franklin, one of the noblest things I ever knew in my life. It makes one's heart beat high, with a sort of sacred joy." [31] The reasons why Lady Franklin sent this to Dickens are uncertain, but it seems possible that knowing of his sympathetic interest and influential position, she consulted or informed him about the appeals. In any event, Dickens continued to value the ideal that he felt was embodied in the Arctic explorers. His remark about his heart beating high with "a sort of sacred joy" indicates that he experienced intense,

[28] "Sir John Franklin and His Crews," *Household Words*, February 3, 1855, pp. 12–20.
[29] These appeals are reviewed in "Official Patriotism," *Household Words*, April 25, 1857, pp. 385–390.
[30] Dickens to W. H. Wills, November 27, 1854, *Letters*, II, 607.
[31] Dickens to Forster, April 1856, *Letters*, II, 768.

noble sentiments merely by reading about Richardson and Franklin. During March and April 1856, the experience must have been especially valuable, for that is the same period in which Dickens informed Forster that life was like a burdened journey with few moments of peace or joy.

The original idea for "The Frozen Deep" was conceived in the context of these events. Dickens had become a temporary resident of Paris in October 1855. In late March 1856, Wilkie Collins began a two- or three-week visit. On March 27, Dickens informed W. C. Macready that when Macready arrived the first week in April, he would find the Dickens family alone, "except that the son of Collins the painter (who writes a good deal in Household Words) dines with us every day." [32] As this remark suggests, Collins, at the time, was neither a popular novelist nor so close a friend to Dickens as he was to become later. He had published three novels, none of them very successful, and had written the script for "The Lighthouse," which he had been unable to sell. He was best known for his articles and stories published in *Bentley's Miscellany* and *Household Words*. Dickens had met him in 1851 when Collins performed a minor role in Bulwer-Lytton's *Not So Bad as We Seem*. From that time on, Collins had become a frequent companion, touring Switzerland and Italy with Dickens and Augustus Egg in 1853, visiting Dickens at his home, and making numerous contributions to *Household Words*, including stories for the 1854 and 1855 Christmas numbers. His visit in March was probably social, but he and Dickens apparently discussed Collins' contributions to *Household Words*. On April 1 Dickens informed Wills that Collins ought to be paid £50, because Collins was "a careful and good writer" on whom they could rely for "Xmas Nos. and the

[32] *Letters*, II, 754.

like" and because Collins was receiving offers from other periodi-
cals which made it "additionally desirable" that Dickens and
Wills "should not shave close in such a case." [33]

The idea for a play based on the Arctic expeditions seems to
have been conceived during Collins' visit. Five days after writing
to Wills about Collins' contributions, Dickens again wrote to
him:

Collins and I have a mighty original notion (mine in the beginning)
for another play at Tavistock House. I propose opening on Twelfth
Night, the theatrical season of that great establishment. But now a
tremendous question. Is Mrs. Wills game to do a Scotch Housekeeper, in a supposed country-house with Mary, Katey, Georgina,
etc. If she can screw her courage up to saying Yes, that country
house opens the piece in a singular way, and that Scotch housekeeper's part shall flow from the present pen. If she says No (but she
won't), no Scotch Housekeeper can be. The Tavistock House Season of 4 nights pauses for a reply. Scotch song (new and original) of
Scotch Housekeeper, would pervade the piece.[34]

This letter makes one point quite clear. By April 6, plans for
"The Frozen Deep" had been developed in some detail. The
setting for Act I had already been determined, and Dickens
knew enough about the action that he could begin planning his
cast, call Act I "singular" or unusual, and imply that a new and
original Scotch song would serve some essential function. It
seems unlikely that details like these could have been settled
unless some plans had been formulated for the more important
Acts II and III. One cannot be certain what was "mighty

[33] *Letters,* II, 754. Walter Dexter's note says that £50 was paid to
Collins for "A Rogue's Life," which appeared March 1 to March 29,
1856, in *Household Words.* In 1855, Collins had been paid £40 for a
similar story, "Sister Rose."

[34] April 6, 1856, *Letters,* II, 755–756.

original" about the "notion" that Dickens had conceived, for there is no direct evidence about the notion except that contained in this letter.

Circumstantial evidence, however, suggests that the notion was associated with Dickens' faith in the nature of men, and with his idea of a natural though unconventional hero. On January 20, he had written to Forster:

Again I am beset by my former notions of a book whereof the whole story shall be on the top of the Great St. Bernard. As I accept and reject ideas for Little Dorrit, it perpetually comes back to me. Two or three years hence, perhaps you'll find me living with the Monks and the Dogs a whole winter—among the blinding snows that fall about that monastery. I have a serious idea that I shall do it, if I live.[35]

This reference suggests the setting of *No Thoroughfare*, which Dickens and Collins wrote as the Christmas number for *All the Year Round* in 1867 and later rewrote as a play. But it indicates, also, that Dickens in 1856 was interested in the association between arctic conditions and monasteries. This association may have implied a moral idea to Dickens, whose heart had leaped with a "sort of sacred joy" as he read about the manly friendship between Richardson and Franklin. Further, Dickens approved the publication in February 1857 of an article that specifically associated the explorers with monks. Again emphasizing the circumstantial nature of Dr. Rae's report and the debt due to the explorers, who embodied values sacred to the British tradition, the article asserted:

Shut up in Arctic monasteries, with no monkish souls, men have learnt energetically to respect and help each other, to trust in each other, and have faith in God. The entire series of books written by Arctic sailors, except only one or two, bears most emphatic witness to

[35] January 20, 1856, *Letters*, II, 734–735.

the fine spirit of manhood nourished among those who bear in company the rigours of the frozen sea.[36]

Although Henry Morley wrote this, the article expresses essentially the same view of "the nature of the men" that Dickens himself expressed in 1854 and undoubtedly continued to hold. The pejorative "monkish souls" probably ought not to be identified with any particular conventional religion. The implied contrast seems to be that between any restrictive, authoritarian moral view, including the smooth gentleman's hypocritical ethic, and the free, noble view arising from a good man's heart. The central issue of "The Frozen Deep" focuses on the nature of Richard Wardour's heart. It seems quite possible that Collins and Dickens had discussed his characterization and that his character and role were among the "mighty original" features of the notion.

Dickens anticipated no difficulty in working with Collins, who was both unconventional and quick to take Dickens' suggestions. Before Collins arrived in Paris, Dickens had written to Wills, "I think I have a good idea for a series of Paris papers into which I can infuse a good deal of myself, if Collins comes here (as I think he will) for some time."[37] In a letter to Collins five days later, Dickens indicated that the series was to be based on the Catacombs and the guillotine.[38] The implication of both letters is that Dickens could not spare the time from *Little Dorrit* to write the articles and that consequently he planned to supply some ideas for articles Collins might write. They seem to have held joint possession of the "mighty original notion" in this sense. From the beginning, they had planned that Collins would

[36] "The Lost English Sailors," *Household Words,* February 14, 1857, pp. 145–147.

[37] January 14, 1856, *Letters,* II, 728.

[38] January 19, 1856, *Letters,* II, 732–734. This series was not written.

write the script while living with Dickens for "some time." The day that Collins returned to England, Dickens wrote to him, "The Pavilion of the Moulineaux I shall, of course, reserve for your summer occupation and work. Talking of which latter, I am reminded to say that the Scotch housekeeper is secured." [39] Collins' summer occupation and work was to be the writing of the script while he lived in France with Dickens.

Even without the script, Dickens knew enough about the general nature of the play to begin interesting others in its production. On May 13, 1856, he wrote to Miss Angela Burdett-Coutts:

I am not without hope . . . that you and Mrs. Brown may be induced to take some interest in what I dare say you never saw—the growth of a play from the beginning. Mr. Collins and I have hammered out a curious idea for a new one, which he is to write, and which we purpose, please God, to bring out on Charley's birthday. Mr. Stanfield has already been hanging out of the centre back-window of the schoolroom at the risk of his life, inventing wonderful effects and measuring the same. [40]

That Dickens sought the interest of Miss Coutts is particularly significant, for he valued her esteem and knew that she disliked his theatrical activities. [41] He hoped that despite her dislike of his earlier activities, she would approve his efforts in producing the new play. The Duke of Devonshire was encouraged, also, to take an interest in it. Dickens wrote him, "If I can only persuade you to see it from a special arm-chair, and can only make you wretched, my satisfaction will be intense." [42]

---

[39] April 13, 1856, *Letters*, II, 757–758.   [40] *Letters*, II, 773–774.
[41] For a discussion of Miss Coutts's general attitude, see *The Heart of Charles Dickens: As Revealed in His Letters to Angela Burdett-Coutts*, ed. Edgar Johnson (New York, 1952), p. 332.
[42] July 5, 1856, *Letters*, II, 785–786.

The plans for the summer work had called for Collins to take up residence with Dickens in July. But Collins was delayed in England. On July 13, Dickens wrote him:

We are all sorry that you are not coming until the middle of next month, but we hope that you will then be able to remain, so that we may all come back together about the Tenth of October. I think (recreation allowed, etc.) that the play will take that time to write. The ladies of the *dram. pers.* are frightfully anxious to get it under way, and to see you locked up in the pavilion.[43]

Even with the delay, Dickens hoped that he would be able to work with Collins for two months on the script. Being familiar with the details of the Arctic expeditions, knowing the limitations of the amateur cast, having had Stanfield's advice on the effects, and having much previous experience as a manager and actor, Dickens could have helped Collins greatly during this two-month period.

Collins came on August 15. Instead of having two months with Dickens, however, Collins could not have had more than about two weeks, for an outbreak of cholera forced the Dickens family to return to England at the end of August.[44] Though much shorter than Dickens and Collins had expected, this work period must have exercised a determinative effect on the script. Each had had four months to think about the "mighty original notion" and Dickens had had an opportunity to discuss the essential stage effects with Stanfield. Unfortunately, there is no direct evidence to indicate precisely what occurred during this period. It is not even certain that Collins had written any part of the script while staying with Dickens, for he may have written the entire script after the two returned to England.

[43] *Letters,* II, 791.
[44] Edgar Johnson, *Charles Dickens: His Tragedy and Triumph* (2 vols.; New York, 1952), II, 865.

Circumstantial evidence, however, indicates that Dickens contributed to Collins' original draft. On September 16, 1856, Dickens informed W. H. Wills that he wanted to hire Collins as a regular contributor to *Household Words*, instead of continuing to pay him by the article or story.

I have been thinking a good deal about Collins, and it strikes me that the best thing we can just now do for H. W. is to add him on to Morley, and offer him Five Guineas a week. He is very suggestive, and exceedingly quick to take my notions. Being industrious and reliable besides, I don't think we should be at an additional expense of £20 in the year by the transaction.[45]

Collins, in October and November 1855, had written "The Ostler" for the *Household Words* Christmas number, *The Holly-Tree Inn*.[46] After that time, he and Dickens had collaborated on nothing except "The Frozen Deep." One may reasonably assume, then, that Dickens was thinking primarily about his work with Collins on the script when he wrote to Wills. Dickens' emphasis in the letter is significant. The principal reason that he gives for wanting to hire Collins is not his competence as a writer—or even his industry and reliability, which are mentioned only as reinforcing arguments. From Dickens' point of view, Collins' principal usefulness as a writer lay in the fact that Collins was "very suggestive" and "exceedingly quick" to take Dickens' "notions." On the basis of circumstantial evidence in this and two additional letters, one may conclude, as does Edgar Johnson, that while Collins was planning the script, he was receiving a "stream of eager suggestions" from Dickens.[47]

About a week after Dickens returned to England, he wrote two letters to Collins. These letters are very important for two

---

[45] *Letters,* II, 800.
[46] "The Ostler," *Household Words,* Christmas, 1855, pp. 9–18.
[47] *Charles Dickens,* II, 865.

reasons. First, they provide the only clues to the kind of suggestions that Dickens had been giving and to the kind of agreement
that he, as manager and principal actor, and Collins, as author of
the script, had reached regarding the general effect the play
ought to achieve. Second, they foreshadow a serious misunderstanding about this effect, a misunderstanding that is revealed by
the number and by the kind of revisions which Dickens later
made in the script to implement his "original notion."

From Tavistock House on September 12, Dickens wrote to
Collins:

An admirable idea. It seems to me to supply and include everything the play wanted. But it is so very strong that I doubt whether
the man can (without an anti-climax) be shown to be rescued and
alive, until the last act. The struggle, the following him away, the
great suspicion, and the suspended interest, in the second. The relief
and joy of the discovery, in the third.

Here, again, Mark's part seems to me to be suggested. An honest,
bluff man, previously admiring and liking me—conceiving the terrible suspicion—watching its growth in his own mind—and gradually
falling from me in the very generosity and manhood of his nature—
would be engaging in itself, would be what he would do remarkably
well, would give me capital things to do with him (and you know
we go very well together), and would greatly strengthen the suspended interest aforesaid.

I throw this out with all deference, of course, to your internal view
and preconception of the matter. Turn it how you will, the strength
of the situation is *prodigious;* and if we don't bring the house down
with it, I'm a—Tory (an illegible word which I mean for T-O-R-Y).

Hoping to see you to-night.[48]

The "admirable idea" evidently refers to Nurse Esther's second
sight. This device is the only "idea" in the script that could be

[48] *Letters,* II, 798–799.

described as "very strong" and that could be used to show "the man" alive at a point early enough to endanger the climax of Act II. In 1866, when Collins was free to use the idea as he wished, he dramatized a man-alive scene. Having eliminated Nurse Esther from the play, Collins gave second sight to Clara Burnham, and ended Act I with a scene which showed Clara huddled with the other women on one side of the stage, and Wardour, a gun in his hand, standing over the prostrate figure of Aldersley on the other. The two men were illuminated by a blood-red light which slowly spread toward Clara as she exclaimed about the "vision" and her guilt.

Dickens judged the idea "admirable" because it solved a serious problem. Act I required that controlled suspense and tension be introduced among the women as preparation for the main action which follows. If those "who take the nearest and dearest interest in the fate of that unfortunate expedition" were shown merely waiting, little in the act would evoke an audience's interest or sympathy. To suggest a parallel between the stage situation and that of the women who waited for news of the Franklin expedition, it was desirable that this tension not be introduced by means of a message from the expedition itself. The "Scotch song (new and original) of Scotch Housekeeper," which Dickens mentioned on April 6, was probably intended to heighten the suspense. It was to "pervade the piece" and could have been written so that its tune and words increased the women's anxiety. Nurse Esther had no song, but she did have second sight, of a sort, and used it to heighten the tension steadily. This trait of character was preferable to a song, which would have been extrinsic to the action. As used in the 1866 version, however, it destroyed the increasing tension in Act II. The "vision" made second sight credible, so that the audience already knew the central issue toward which Act II moved. Crayford and Wardour were reduced to fulfilling expectations. After the blood-red vision scene, Wardour could do little to heighten the suspense. This anticlimax was bad enough when the conventional romantic heroine anticipated his most powerful scene; it would have been worse if Nurse Esther, a minor character, had had credible visions.

Dickens recognized the danger so clearly that he reviewed for Collins the general effects already decided upon. In the context of the comments about Mark Lemon's part (Lt. Crayford) and of "the great suspicion . . . in the second," the phrase "suspended interest" can refer only to the question of how Wardour will act in his moment of greatest temptation. The phrase "following him away" reveals the importance that Dickens placed on Wardour, for he might more logically have said "them," referring either to all the men who leave at the end of Act II or to Aldersley and Wardour as a pair. The absence of the characters' names makes it highly probable that the details for Act II had not been determined. But Dickens clearly wanted the act to focus the audience's attention on Wardour. Since the "suspended interest" was to depend on Wardour's action rather than on Aldersley's fate, Dickens evidently expected the "relief and joy" in Act III to spring primarily from the discovery that Wardour in his moment of greatest stress had lived up to a noble code of conduct, thus meriting the love, admiration, and pity that Crayford, Aldersley, and Clara expressed for him at the end of the play.

Dickens reviewed the function assigned to Mark Lemon only because Collins' proposed use of second sight conflicted with this function and threatened to spoil its relation to the "suspended interest." This function centered on the issue of the faith in the nature of man. Dickens emphasized the "growth," or gradual development, of the "terrible suspicion," which was to come as a result of the "very generosity and manhood" of Crayford's nature. Because of his own goodness, Crayford would gradually lose faith in Wardour, who, although he could weep when Crayford first met him, would be so frozen by hate at the end of Act II that he could be totally indifferent to the fate of his comrades, attack his only friend, and plan cold-blooded murder. Dickens wanted this "terrible suspicion" that Wardour was going to destroy himself by murdering Aldersley to climax Act II, and he wanted it dramatized as the loss of one man's faith in another, not as a preternatural vision.

Dickens and Collins apparently did meet on the night of the twelfth, for the next day Dickens had more information about Act I. On September 13, he wrote to Collins:

Another idea I have been waiting to impart. I dare say you have anticipated it. *Now,* Mrs. Wills's second sight is clear as to the illustration of it, and greatly helps that suspended interest. Thus: "You ask *me* what I see of those lost Voyagers. I see the lamb in the grasp of the lion—your bonnie bird alone with the hawk. What do I see? I see you and all around you crying, Blood! The stain of his blood is upon you!"

Which would be right to a certain extent, and absolutely wrong as to the marrow of it.[49]

Collins accepted this dialogue, using it as Nurse Esther's final speech to conclude Act I. His acceptance indicates just how specific some of Dickens' suggestions may have been throughout the planning stage and how much Dickens may have affected the original draft, even in small details.

How much Dickens may have affected it and how much he did affect it are rather different issues. As Dickens acknowledged on September 12, his suggestions were subject to Collins' "internal view and preconception of the matter." Even if Collins strove to satisfy Dickens, he could not have had exactly the same

[49] *Letters,* II, 799.

internal view and preconceptions that Dickens had. The use that
Collins proposed for his "admirable idea" threatened the central
effects which Dickens regarded as essential to "the matter."
Collins' proposal indicates the possibility of a basic misunderstanding. Dickens' *"Now,"* in the September 13 letter, indicates
that Dickens thought that Collins shared his view. He would
hardly have written to Wills three days later about Collins'
being "very suggestive" and "exceedingly quick" to take his
"notions" if he had thought Collins confused about essential
effects. Although Collins may have wanted to satisfy Dickens
and Dickens may have thought Collins able to satisfy him, the
possibility of a misunderstanding remained.

In France, Collins and Dickens could have consulted daily
about the script. In England, they could not. They lived miles
apart and the forced move had threatened Dickens' work on
Little Dorrit, which, of course, was much more important to him
than his work on the play. To Miss Coutts on September 26,
Dickens explained the circumstances that would have discouraged frequent consultations about the script:

I have come home to such an immense arrear of demands on my
attention, that I am falling behind-hand with that reserve of Little
Dorrit which has kept me easy during its progress, and to lose which
would be a serious thing. All the week I have been hard at it with a
view to tomorrow; but I have not been in a quick vein (which is not
to be commanded), and have made but tardy way. If I stick to it
resolutely now, next week will bring me up. If I let a day go now,
there is no saying when I may work round again and come right.[50]

Collins and Dickens do not seem to have consulted frequently at
any time while Collins was actually writing the script. The
letters suggest that they had discussed the general effects in some

[50] *Letters,* II, 802.

detail, including the setting and characterizations, but that Collins was left the task of writing the dialogue and creating the situations that were to implement these effects. It is significant that Dickens had not mentioned the name of a single character. In the absence of a script, neither he nor Collins could have known how well Collins understood Dickens' "notions," regardless of his readiness to accept them. Dickens apparently saw the script for the first time on October 2, when Collins arrived at Tavistock House "in a breathless state, with the first two acts of his play in three." [51]

Dickens praised Collins' play and said nothing about any serious inadequacies in the script, but he extensively revised these first two acts, and later Act III. On October 9, he informed Collins that he had been revising the script during the past week, but dissembled as to the number and kind of the revisions.

I should like to show you some cuts I have made in the second act (subject to authorial sanction, of course). They are mostly verbal, and all bring the Play closer together.

Also, I should like to know whether it is likely that you will want to alter anything in these two acts. If not, here are Charley, Mark, and I, all ready to write, and we may get a fair copy out of hand. From said fair copy all my people will write out their own parts.

. . . . .

I am more sure than ever of the effect.[52]

The phrases "some cuts" and "mostly verbal" are misleading. Some of the cuts are "mostly verbal," but there are more than "some" suggests. More important, Dickens made other cuts and additions that cannot be described as "mostly verbal" because

---

[51] Dickens to Miss Coutts, October 3, 1856, *Letters*, II, 802.
[52] *Letters*, II, 805.

they do considerably more than merely increase the pace. They protect Wardour's central place and the "suspended interest" about which Dickens had been concerned in September.

Dickens' dissembling about the number and kind of changes can be explained as his courteous attempt to avoid offending a younger and less able colleague. If a disagreement had arisen Dickens might have deferred to Collins' "authorial sanction," but he might have been surprised if Collins had chosen to exercise it. He had been surprised when Mrs. Gaskell objected to his revisions of *North and South,* and he had commented scornfully to Collins about her objections to his having taken out "the stiflings—hard-plungings, lungeings [sic], and other convulsions . . . and her weakenings and damagings of her own effects." [53] Collins had just been employed as a regular contributor to *Household Words,* had written the script for Dickens to use, and had less experience in the theater than Dickens had. The public reputations of both would be involved in the performances. As manager, Dickens had to synthesize the various elements, including the script, to make these performances effective. He, not Collins, knew the talents and shortcomings of the amateur cast, whose most important members he had selected before receiving the script. As manager, Dickens tailored the script so that it could be used to attain the effect which he thought desirable and for which he would bear the primary responsibility.

Collins gave Dickens the script for a relatively conventional melodrama. In Act I, tension was heightened by two devices: the threat of Nurse Esther's effect on Clara and the Nurse's prophecy. The day of the action was the third anniversary of a party that had been given the night before the expedition left for the Arctic. The first scene opened on Rose reading silently from

[53] March 24, 1855, *Letters,* II, 645–646.

a newspaper and informing Mrs. Steventon that it contained no
news to interest them. They then began talking about the anniversary and the dangerous effect that the strange old "Highland
Nurse" was having on Clara Burnham. As they mentioned the
dresses they had worn at the party three years earlier, Lucy
Crayford entered. She informed them that she was vividly aware
of the anniversary and that, if she had not been, the "accident"
of just having seen the dress she had worn would have reminded
her of the date. The three women talked about the dresses and
again about their concern for Clara. From that point on, the
tension evolved from the threat that the Highland Nurse posed
to her young mistress. Clara revealed only to Lucy her knowledge that her rival lovers were together in the missing expedition and her fear that Wardour would harm Aldersley if
"chance" uncovered his identity as the rival. A series of speeches
prepared for Nurse Esther's fateful "tidings." This series was
introduced by "A Voice," which was obviously Nurse Esther's.
By designating the speaker thus, Collins apparently intended
that her first speeches would be uttered off-stage, where she
would have had no opportunity to overhear the revealing conversation between Clara and Lucy, which immediately preceded
the dialogue spoken by "A Voice." This staging would have
suggested that Nurse Esther's "tidings" came from a credible
power of vision, that she had a preternatural power giving her
information which confirmed Clara's fears. The act ended with
Lucy appealing to Providence for protection and with Clara in
grave danger of losing her sanity or her faith in a merciful God.
This development is similar to the one Collins used in the
narrative version, in which, however, he dramatized the party
scene and attributed the power of second sight to Clara.

Act II opened with Lt. Crayford calling attention to a strange
sound outside the Arctic hut with the word "Hark," the same

word Nurse Esther had used at the end of Act I to introduce her fateful tidings. He sent Darker, who had a gun, to see whether a bear had been prowling near the hut. Later, Aldersley, the conventional romantic hero, called Wardour "the bear of the expedition." As the scene progressed, the noble Aldersley, though weakened by illness, defied a brutish Wardour, who had begun slyly to threaten Aldersley after learning his identity. The act ended by dramatizing a strong affection between Aldersley and Crayford. Wardour was set apart from them and from the departing members of the expedition as a villain. Crayford appealed to heaven for help, as had his sister at the end of Act I. The action as a whole confirmed the threat revealed by the Nurse.

When the two groups, the women and the men, were brought together in Act III, the principal interest was directed toward Clara, as it had been in Act I. The two groups shared bits of their information; much of the dialogue described events that the audience had already seen dramatized. Nurse Esther, who found her prophecy confirmed by the absence of Wardour and Aldersley, continued to be a grave threat to Clara. Most of the act moved toward a scene in which Lucy told Crayford the details of the prophecy, and he told her the details of Wardour's and Aldersley's departure. Both then realized that because all the men on the expedition knew that Wardour and Aldersley left together, Clara was certain to learn this and to interpret it as confirming the prophecy and her own guilt. The confirmation would have terrible, but unspecified, results. Shortly after this scene, there was a luncheon scene interrupted by Wardour's appearing as an unrecognized castaway in rags. Wardour remained a mysterious stranger until Crayford entered, identified him, and accused him of murdering Frank. Collins' stage directions assigned Wardour several maniacal laughs during this action. Clara, who had been kept off-stage, heard Wardour's and Aldersley's names mentioned in loud tones and rushed on-stage. Seeing her, Wardour exclaimed, "Found at last," and rushed off-stage, returning amid cheers with Frank in his arms. After placing Frank at Clara's feet, he withdrew to one side with Crayford, who begged Wardour's forgiveness. Wardour revealed his struggle with the tempter, his conquest of the temptation, and the long struggle, day and night over land and sea, to save Frank. Finally, Frank and Clara joined Crayford at Wardour's side just before he died.

About this action, little could be described as "mighty original," and Dickens' changes suggest that he might have regarded it as "conventional but not natural." [54] Collins' script drew attention to a pair of young lovers, separated but threatened by the same villain. If Lucy's appeal at the end of Act I and Lt. Crayford's at the end of Act II are given any weight, then the young lovers' hopes of circumventing the threat lay in Providence rather than in anything in the villain's nature. The action ended with the lovers reunited, able to live happily ever after with the threat removed. Its one original feature was the "admirable idea" of second sight, which Collins may have taken from Scott's *Redgauntlet*.[55]

It is highly improbable that Dickens would have been excited by this kind of conventional action at any time, much less in

[54] Dickens to Miss King, February 9, 1855, *Letters*, II, 623–624.
[55] In *Redgauntlet*, a Highland story, Wandering Willie tells a tale that could have come either from a preternatural vision or from a drunken imagination—Scott appears to have been deliberately ambiguous. The tune played in Act I when Nurse Esther was identified as a Highland Nurse and again when she entered was entitled "Wandering Willie." For Scott's tale, see "Letter XI"; for the tune, "Wandering Willie," which identified the blind fiddler, Wandering Willie, see "Chapter IX: Latimer's Journal, in Continuation."

1856. On August 15, the day Collins arrived to begin work on the script, Dickens had condemned conventional heroes as unnatural analogues of men. This condemnation, Dickens' concern about the "suspended interest" in Wardour, the foreshadowing of "lion" and "hawk" in the dialogue Dickens wrote for Nurse Esther, and many of his revisions, suggest that Dickens had a different "notion" than Collins as to the "mighty original" element in the play. Dickens apparently wanted Wardour, the logical choice for the villain in a conventional action, to be the unconventional but natural hero. Wardour could have "the experiences, trials, perplexities, and confusions inseparable from the making or unmaking of all men." Further, by enduring through these, Wardour could reveal his heroic stature, and the resilient strength of the noble sentiments in the depth of his heart. But Wardour could make these climactic revelations effectively only if the preceding action had prepared properly for his death scene.

In Act I Dickens undercut the conventional love interest and the sentimental pity for the suffering heroine by minimizing the threat to Clara Burnham and subtly heightening the threat to the entire expedition. He reversed the order of speakers so that Mrs. Steventon, the older woman, could have the newspaper, and he wrote the dialogue rendered as her reading from the newspaper, which contains figurative overtones of "Fortune," "Ariel," "Sisters," and the abandoned "Hope." He added the stage direction for Mrs. Steventon to repress a shudder as she broke off this reading. The effect was to dramatize the danger to all the members of the Arctic expedition and the anxiety of all the women who waited for them. This change prevented the first tension in the act arising as anxiety about Clara, and it emphasized the more important and more natural anxiety about the missing men. He cut several later speeches in which Clara talked about her guilty anxiety and in which Lucy Crayford urged, at times begged, her not to worry.

Finally, Dickens modified the device of second sight throughout, so that it could be viewed as a dangerous superstition or as a preternatural power. He weakened the romantic suggestions evoked by a strange, old Highland Nurse, who threatened "Southron ladies" with a foreboding prophecy in reasonably correct English. He wrote the dialogue that designates Nurse Esther as "Scotch" and as "Lowland by usage and education," and he revised all of her speeches so that she would use heavy dialect and vulgarisms like "deary" and "Missy." [56] For Collins' "A Voice," Dickens substituted her name and changed the stage directions so that the audience would see her in a position to overhear the last part of Clara's and Lucy's revealing conversation. The audience could infer that Nurse Esther got the information about Frank's danger and Clara's guilt by eavesdropping. He cut altogether several of her speeches, and speeches in which Lucy or Clara were excessively disturbed by her. In particular, he cut Lucy's appeal to Providence. The general effect of these modifications was to simplify the roles and to prevent the tension reaching such a height that it would destroy the effect of the tension rising from Wardour's later actions and the "growth" of Lt. Crayford's "terrible suspicion." Anxiety was proper for Act I, but terror had to be reserved for the climactic scenes in Act II.

[56] The difference between "Highland" and "Lowland" seems like the difference between English and Cockney. On April 6, Dickens had specified a "Scotch Housekeeper"; Collins did not use the word "Scotch" anywhere in his original script. Both "Scotch" and dialect had pejorative suggestions for Dickens. Comparing an impending visit with the Hogarths to "what would be called in a popular musical entertainment 'the flick o' our ain firesides,' " Dickens announced that he was "dead sick of the Scottish tongue in all its moods and tenses" (to Collins, March 24, 1855, *Letters*, II, 645–646).

To protect the "suspended interest," Dickens made similar changes in Act II. He cut the reference to the bear from Crayford's and Darker's speeches in the opening scene, took the gun away from Darker, and wrote the transitional dialogue, which still permitted the door to be opened so that the audience could see the British ensign on the backdrop, but which emphasized Crayford's concern only with the familiar weather and duty. This emphasis, along with John Want's humorous speeches, suggested that although the men lacked the comforts of home dramatized in Act I, they were not in the sort of imminent peril prophesied by Nurse Esther. The Arctic cold and wastes threatened them, but their spirits were good, as were their chances for survival or rescue. In later scenes, Dickens developed the suggestions of the dialogue that he had written for Nurse Esther on September 13. "Lion" and "hawk" appropriately foreshadowed Wardour's development as a strong man capable of murder because cold hate had frozen his noble sentiments, but also as a man with potential nobility of sentiment and character. That he had had this nobility and sentiment in the past was made clear by the scene in which Crayford reminded him of their shipboard meeting, when Wardour had been shedding tears. This permitted Crayford to validate the statement he had made earlier about Wardour's having a great and generous heart, by encouraging Wardour to review his previous exploits in the fever swamps of Africa in the service of a love that was more courtly than biblical, despite Wardour's reference to Jacob. Wardour's indifference to the fate of his comrades had been a source of anxiety to Crayford, and Wardour's willed decision never again to shed tears heightened this anxiety because it revealed the "icebound" condition of Wardour's soul. To undercut further the brutish suggestions in the original draft, Dickens gave Wardour the gun and designated him as the bear hunter. "Lamb" and "bonnie bird" foreshadowed Aldersley's development as a nice, but sickly young man, who could be carried to the feet of his sweetheart by the lion, whose thawed heart eventually made him gentle toward the lamb. Dickens cut a few scenes in which Wardour slyly threatened Aldersley after his identity had been revealed by the carving on the bed, and in which Aldersley nobly defied the petty threats. After these changes, Aldersley's designation of Wardour as the "bear" of the expedition suggested merely a petulant misunderstanding of Wardour's character.

Wardour became not less dangerous than "bear" suggested, but more dangerous. In Collins' version there was a clutter of action near the end of Act II, in which Wardour was set apart from Crayford as a conventional villain and in which the force of his threat to Aldersley was lost. Dickens' revisions of this scene will be shown in detail later. In general, he changed the action to make Wardour's threat to Aldersley much more intense. But Dickens also restored the relation between Crayford and Wardour, which had concerned him in the September 12 letter. Crayford reminded Wardour, and the audience, of the earlier scene in which Wardour's innate greatness and generosity had been discussed. Because of this innate nobility, Crayford could pity Wardour despite his indifference to his comrades, his attack on his only friend, and his open threat to murder Aldersley. In the performances, this scene evoked terror. Aldersley had been too weak and insignificant to command strong sympathy; Wardour had not. The primary threat was that if Wardour murdered Aldersley, Wardour would have committed an irrevocable action, destroying himself as well as Aldersley. After Dickens' revisions, Wardour emerged as more dangerous, but as less villainous. Because his "soul" or noble sentiment was "ice-bound"—the metaphor in the Prologue designating the condition of Wardour's inner life—Wardour might murder Aldersley, but Wardour had no ignoble, petty, sly malice in his nature.

With the notion that Dickens wanted to implement, Act III presented an interesting problem. Like the preceding acts, it had to prepare for the revelation of the final state of Wardour's soul after the "passage at its northern pole" had been found. The discovery could not easily be dramatized because it was to come as the result of a convulsive movement within the depths of Wardour's heart and to be followed by long struggles over the snow, ice, and sea, day and night. In the narrative version, Collins tried to dramatize the "temptation" in the Arctic wastes, but did not attempt to dramatize the climactic change.[57] In 1857, the final action had to center on Wardour; yet Wardour could not be allowed on stage until the final moments of Act III. To prepare for these moments, Dickens modified the conventional device for maintaining suspense, a young girl in peril, on which Collins had centered the interest in Act III

Collins had made Nurse Esther a major threat in Act III just as he had in Act I. After Dickens revised Act II, the ambiguous preternatural suggestions, desirable for heightening suspense in Act I, would only disrupt the terror to be evoked in Act III by Wardour's disordered, but "natural," passions. Dickens destroyed the ambiguity, partly by radically cutting scenes in which Nurse Esther threatened and other characters took her threats seriously, and by making explicit the suggestions he had introduced near the end of Act I. Dickens wrote most of John Want's third speech, which begins, "She's only a cracked old woman." This dialogue emphasized that second sight was a peculiarly "Scotch" superstition, that Nurse Esther did not have even common sense, and that she got the material for her so-called prophecies by picking up "bits" of information and piecing them together. The music, "Spoilt Child," which followed this speech may have emphasized her petulant immaturity, her childish desire to call attention to herself by affecting to have a preternatural power giving her special information.[58] Dickens also wrote all the heavy dialect for her speeches as he had in Act I.

By minimizing the preternatural threat, Dickens emphasized the natural and more credible threat that Clara would learn from one of the officers that Wardour and Aldersley had disappeared together. Sensing Clara's fear of such an event, Crayford had lied when the men and women had come together, letting the women believe that Wardour had died in the hut and that Aldersley had been lost during the search expedition. This construction of events allowed Clara to feel free from any guilt toward either Wardour or Aldersley and to hope that Aldersley somehow might have survived. It also minimized the immediate threat to her and maintained Wardour's unknown action in the frozen wastes as the principal source of tension.

To dramatize his heroic struggles and to prepare for his almost immediate death, Wardour had to be shown at the extreme of physical and mental exhaustion. For Collins' conventional version, this presented no problems. The brutish Wardour of Act II could be, and was, presented as a maniac giving several conventional insane laughs. With the principal interest drawn to the reunited lovers, Wardour could die a pitiable man, who had

---

[58] John Want uses "second hand eye" scornfully to designate Nurse Esther's garbled interpretation. In the first Franklin article, Dickens used "second hand" to designate what he regarded as a garbled interpretation of hearsay evidence.

justly sacrificed his physical strength to save the noble Aldersley. Dickens cut these scenes radically, rearranged the stage action, and wrote several important transitional speeches. He deleted speeches in which Crayford accused Wardour of being a "villain" or a "ruthless villain" and in which Lucy echoed the accusations. In Collins' draft Wardour exclaimed "Let me go!" and laughed as the others on stage shrank away from him; otherwise he had nothing to do during Crayford's accusation. Dickens left one "villain" reference in Crayford's dialogue, deleted Lucy's echoes and Wardour's laughs, and wrote some new dialogue. The following is the most important part of this new dialogue:

Wardour: Villain? And where is Frank? Ah! I think I know your meaning. I think I dimly understand.

Crayford: (*To them all*) Look at this conscience-stricken wretch! Confess, unhappy ruin of a man! Tell us how it was done.

The effect of such changes was to avoid the dehumanizing suggestions of "maniac" in the modern sense of "psychotic." Crayford recognized Wardour as a formerly good man apparently ruined by his own conscience. Although Wardour's reason was still shaken in the revised script, Wardour could respond to Crayford's accusation not with laughs suggesting total loss of reason, but with a speech indicating that he understood Crayford's just error. He understood what Crayford said and why he said it. The changes emphasized Wardour's importance in relation to the others, left him enough reason to make credible his following recognition of, and response to, Clara, killed the suggestions of brutish horror, and evoked limited pity for, as well as fear of, Wardour. Even when Wardour seemed a murderer and was physically and mentally exhausted, he retained enough control and dignity to appear moments later as a self-sacrificing hero.

The script for Wardour's death scene did not require major changes. Dickens shortened speeches in which Crayford begged forgiveness; these detracted, both by their length and by their emphasis on Crayford's remorse, from Wardour's revelation of his suffering and his affirmation of the victory of noble sentiments. Dickens removed two short speeches by Crayford and moved one of Wardour's so that Clara would clearly attend to Frank's feet as a direct response to Wardour's remark about Frank's being "footsore." Although relatively minor, such changes increased Wardour's importance by suggesting that he controlled the action in the closing moments of the play. They helped to make sensible the curious device of hiding the conventional heroine and hero amidst the minor characters at one side of the stage, for, like Dickens' preceding changes, they helped to make the play Wardour's.

Partly because Dickens changed the draft often by cutting rather than by rewriting, the exact effect of such revisions is difficult to describe. The parallel scripts for the scene that ended Act II offer a typical example of such an effect. The new dialogue and stage directions added in Dickens' handwriting have been italicized to make the comparison easier. Collins' draft is very rough because of changes that both he and Dickens made in it. The script for it given below cannot be regarded as absolutely definitive.

Collins' Draft	Dickens' Revised Script
Crayford: (To Wardour) I said to you a little while ago there were times when a man is	Crayford: I said to you, *Wardour*, a little while ago, there *are* times when a man is to be

to be pitied. I pity you now.
Take your hand away.

Wardour: (Releasing him) I
beg your pardon.

Frank: Like a Brave Man!
Come along!

(The men of the Sea-Mew
file out, equipped for the journey from the inner hut, and join
their comrades outside.)

The Captain of the Wan-
derer: The spare snow shoes, the
staff, and the furs for Mr. Wardour, who joins the exploring
party.

(Exit. A sailor enters and
equips Wardour.)

Crayford: (Taking Frank
aside) Once more!—be ruled by
me. Look! There is a snow storm
gathering. Stay, Frank—stay!

Frank: Anything else to please
you, Crayford—anything but
stopping here.

Wardour: Why indeed? Who
talks of stopping here!

Crayford: Stay, Frank—stay!
Remember how weak you are!

Wardour: Weak! What then?
Suppose he slips into a snow-
drift—here's an arm to pull him
out. (Offers his arm to Frank.)

Crayford: Don't take it Frank!

Wardour: (To Frank) Does

pitied. I pity you, now. Take
your hand away.

Wardour: (Releasing him) I
beg your pardon.

Frank: Like a brave man!
Come along!

he think you are afraid of me?
(Offers his arm)
Frank: Afraid! (A pause.
Frank and Wardour look at each
other steadily.) If this is another
of your jokes, I would not rec-
ommend you to make it again.
Afraid! Here is my answer!
(Takes Wardour's arm)
Wardour: Away, then! Away
over the snow and the ice. Away
over the road that no human
footsteps have trodden.
Frank: (At the door with
Wardour) God bless you Cray-
ford!

(The men outside move off,
leaving Frank and Wardour
alone.)
Crayford: (Rushing up to
him and seizing his hand)
God preserve you, Frank. I
would give all I have in the
world to be with you. (Wardour
offers his hand.) No! not till the
march is over, not till the rescue
has come, not till I see Frank
Aldersley again! (Turns back
into the hut, then looks round.
Frank waves his hand.) Keep
with the main body, Frank!
Wardour: (Leading Frank
off) He keeps with me!

Wardour: *Bring me my gun
there! (Bateson brings it.) Come
then! Come over the Snow and
the Ice! Come over the road that
no human footsteps have ever
trodden, and where no human
trace is ever left! (Loads his gun,
and rams the charge home.)*
Frank: (At the door) God
bless you, Crayford!
(The men outside move off,
leaving Frank *alone in the
snow.*)
Crayford: (*Going* to him, and
seizing his hand) *Heaven* preserve you, Frank! (*They shake
hands, and Frank begins climbing the Drift.*) I would give all I
have in the world to be with
you. *While you can stand,* keep
with the Main Body, Frank!

Wardour: *While he can
stand,* he keeps with Me!

*(Exeunt Wardour and Frank.
Crayford left alone in the Hut
watching them over the snow.)*
End of the Second Act

(Enter Lieutenant Steventon
from the inner hut, with the
men left behind.)

Steventon: They're off! A
cheer, men—give them a cheer
at parting!

(The men obey. An answer-
ing cheer is heard in the distance.)

Steventon: (At the door calling to Crayford) The snow falls
fast, and lies deep. It will be a
hard trial to the weaker men—a
hard trial to Frank.

Crayford: (To himself) Is the
snow Frank's only danger? God
grant it may be so—God grant it!

(A Scene of snow-mist closes
up, and hides the hut from view.
The curtain falls.)

In this concluding scene, Collins made explicit the character
traits foreshadowed in the preceding scenes. Although weakened
by illness, Aldersley bravely defied both the threatening elements and Wardour. His actions dramatized the comparison that
Crayford made, in Act III, between Aldersley and Nelson, asso-
ciating Aldersley rather than Wardour with the traditional hero.
Except in physical strength, Aldersley seemed Wardour's superior. His superiority was confirmed by the strong friendship

between him and Crayford, who scorned Wardour as villainous. Wardour was allowed little action in this important scene. In effect, he was set aside by the friendship between Crayford and Aldersley and lost amid the cheers of the remaining seamen for their deserving comrades. He left the stage as an indifferent villain, unconcerned with the common good in his cowardly pursuit of private vengeance. The slyness of his threats in the former scenes as well as in this one is indicated by Crayford's uncertainty as to whether the villain would be able to harm the hero.

Dickens' cuts and additions gave the ending a rather different effect. The issue became whether Wardour would emerge from the frozen wastes with any "human trace" left within him. Wardour's sly threat and Aldersley's brave defiance were eliminated. Crayford was left an older man's concern for a young and ill comrade, but showed no sign of a strong friendship between them. Crayford was concerned at least as much about Wardour as about Frank. He went to Frank after he had expressed his pity for Wardour, and he went in response to Frank's touching but youthful farewell. Wardour has all of the dramatic dialogue and action in the concluding scene. The gun that Dickens took from Darker in the beginning of the act was given to Wardour, who then had the only gun in the act. Wardour's threat was open and clear. Acting in Collins' draft, Dickens could only have drawn his audience's scorn as Wardour draws Crayford's. With the revised script, Dickens terrified his audiences.

The Staging and the Performances

Having gotten a satisfactory script, Dickens had completed only the first of several tasks essential to implementing his "original notion." Even in producing the children's theatricals, he had done "everybody's work and more, in the course of preparation and rehearsal." [59] These plays, like Collins' "The Lighthouse," had been intended merely to amuse the children and a few family friends. The largest audiences—for "The Lighthouse"—had numbered twenty-five persons. But "The Frozen Deep" was not produced merely as a "lark." It was a serious play with which Dickens hoped to attain a strong effect. Its audiences were to number slightly more than ninety persons and were to include the Chief Justices of England and the President of the Royal Academy. Furthermore, Dickens intended that the performances and the audience's reaction should be publicized, for he invited professional reviewers and encouraged them to comment freely on anything they saw that might be of public interest.

As manager of the amateur company, Dickens assumed the responsibility for every detail of the performance. Both he and the audiences knew that he bore this responsibility, and that prominent people were coming to see a production by Dickens, not a play by Collins. The reviewer for *The Leader* made Dickens' importance clear when he wrote, "Mr. Dickens, moreover, is a genuine manager, 'creating' new pieces, as well as reviving old; and it is a new 'creation' we have now to notice." [60] To achieve this "creation," Dickens had to solve more complex problems than any previous Tavistock House production had

[59] Charles Dickens, Jr., "Reminiscences," p. 19.
[60] January 10, 1857, p. 44.

The Prompt-Book—Page 1

The page contains revisions in both Dickens' and Collins' handwriting, the latter presumably made in 1866. In the first line of the stage directions Dickens added, "A pleasant room in a country-house"; Collins deleted "pleasant" and added "A handsomely-furnished." Other additions to the stage directions are in Collins' hand, as are the additions to Rose's and Mrs. Steventon's second speeches. In the draft from which the prompt-book was made, Dickens had made several changes in the opening dialogue that were overlooked by the copyist (who was probably Charles Dickens, Jr., or Mark Lemon); Dickens changed "Rose beckons" to "Mrs. S. beckons," "Caroline" to "Rose," and "is" to "us." A direction for the prompter, beginning "Before ringing up," is written on the back of the preceding page. (From M.A. 81, Pierpont Morgan Library; reproduced by permission of the Trustees of the Library.)

The Prompt-Book—Page 3

Most of this page is in Dickens' hand, including "(*Exit Maid, with watering-pot, etc.*)." On the back of page 2 Dickens also wrote two stage directions: "(Comes down, takes her work from her work table, and returns with it to tea table)" and "(Re-enter Maid and exit with the bird)." The position for the first is marked by the "X" between "my dear," and "but"; it was evidently intended to replace "(rises, goes to her work table, and takes her work.)," also in Dickens' hand, even though the original direction was not deleted. The position for the second is indicated by the symbol after "Polar Seas." The symbol before "Rose" refers to Collins' revision of the deleted speeches, added on the back of page 2. References to Clara's dreams in Collins' revision indicate that his changes were made in 1866. (From M.A. 81, Pierpont Morgan Library; reproduced by permission of the Trustees of the Library.)

developed. He was bringing an amateur cast before experienced theater-goers. The actors did not present a serious problem, because some had had previous experience and all had been carefully selected. The actresses, however, were inexperienced and were being asked to perform in a situation that might have made even some professional actresses nervous. Dickens had not previously directed a play whose effect depended so heavily on the performances of inexperienced actresses. Finally, the large audiences that Dickens desired created a special problem. To find room for them and for the elaborate spectacle, Dickens had to design and build a stage; then he had to adjust the script and the spectacle to the peculiarities of that stage.

Because of his part in the genesis of the script, Dickens faced relatively few problems with his actors. He had avoided potential problems partly by assigning the only difficult male roles, aside from Wardour's, to the most experienced men and partly by tailoring the roles to fit the natural abilities of the men. He gave the only difficult subordinate roles, those of Lt. Crayford and John Want, to Mark Lemon and Augustus Egg, both of whom he had worked with in several other plays. In his September 12 letter, Dickens had urged Collins to consider Lemon's natural ability while developing Crayford's characterization. Dissatisfied with Collins' development, Dickens retailored the role to fit the idea that he had designated in his letter. Lemon apparently had been chosen in the first place because his temperament harmonized with the "curious idea" that had been "hammered out" by Dickens and Collins. John Oxenford, who had seen the 1857 play, remarked in 1866 that the parts had been so carefully tailored to suit particular men that even excellent professional actors had difficulty with them. As examples, he cited Richard Wardour and John Want. He thought few professionals could attain the "frenzy" that seemed to come naturally to

Dickens or the "quaint misery in the aspect of Augustus Egg," which had made his comic portrayal more effective than that of the professional actor, Dominic Murray.[61] Dickens ought to be credited with effective casting, but he was able to make such suitable selections because he and Collins had planned the whole action with specific persons in mind for the important roles.

Dickens faced more serious problems with the inexperienced actresses, who had to carry the burden of Act I and much of Act III. Georgina Hogarth (Lucy Crayford) was the most experienced of the group, having played a minor role in *Every Man in His Humor* (1851) and the only important female role in "The Lighthouse." Mary Dickens (Clara Burnham), who was only seventeen, had played a minor role in "The Lighthouse." Kate Dickens (Rose Ebsworth), who was only sixteen, had played an even slighter role than Mary's in the farce that followed "The Lighthouse." Helen Hogarth (Mrs. Steventon), Georgina's younger sister, and Mrs. Wills (Nurse Esther) were apparently without any previous acting experience.

Dickens may have considered natural inclinations or abilities with his actresses as he had with the actors. Lucy Crayford, like her brother, is allowed a special relation to Wardour. Having been in love with a man "dead" to her because he is married, she can sympathize with Wardour's disappointment in love. This special relation is prepared for in Act I and dramatized near the end of Act III. Georgina Hogarth, like Mark Lemon, was very fond of Dickens. In later versions, Collins presented Lucy as Lt. Crayford's wife rather than as his sister, deliberately disassociating her from Wardour and drawing both Crayfords closer to the conventional young lovers. In general, however, the women's

[61] *The Times,* October 29, 1866, p. 10.

roles are so slightly developed that they do not seem tailored to fit any particular natural inclinations or abilities.

Dickens worked intensely with his amateur cast to achieve polished performances. For the Tavistock House production, he began rehearsing his own family as early as October 17 and began full-scale rehearsals by November 7.[62] He held at least two rehearsals every week, oftener three and sometimes four.[63] Because of the regularly scheduled entertainment at the Gallery of Illustration, Dickens was unable to use its stage at a reasonable hour. For these later rehearsals, he worked with his amateurs from midnight until four o'clock in the morning.[64] The result of such efforts was surprisingly good. Both before the select Tavistock House audiences and before the later public audiences, the inexperienced women impressed the reviewers as having achieved an extraordinarily natural manner. Only firm, kindly direction and constant practice could have produced such a performance.

While Dickens was directing his amateur cast, he had to solve staging problems not normally associated with his Tavistock House productions. He had determined that the notion should have all the help that spectacle could give it, and he wanted the quality of this spectacle at least to equal that of the professional stage. He bore all the cost and assumed all the trouble that his desire for this quality brought. He remodeled the Tavistock House schoolroom, designing and building a special room in the

[62] Dickens to Rev. Whitwell Elwin, October 17, 1856, *Letters*, II, 807; Dickens to Catherine Dickens, November 7, 1856, in *Mr. and Mrs. Charles Dickens: His Letters to Her*, ed. Kate Perugini and Walter Dexter (London, 1912), p. 253.

[63] Charles Dickens, Jr., "Reminiscences," p. 21.

[64] Elias Bredsdorff, *Hans Andersen and Charles Dickens: A Friendship and Its Dissolution* (Copenhagen, 1956), p. 78.

garden solely for the performances. He supervised stage carpenters and gas fitters, argued with the fire insurance company, and practiced with "Snowboys." He enlisted the aid of, and worked with, two painters, one of them famous, and a young musician, who was to have a distinguished career. Living in the midst of chaos and carrying on the normal duties imposed by *Little Dorrit* and *Household Words,* Dickens communicated his own zeal to his volunteer helpers as he supervised their varied activities.

As producer, Dickens found his first major problem in the schoolroom, which he used as his theater. This large room was rectangular and had a bay window in one side. For previous theatricals, Dickens had seated small audiences in the bay and had placed the scenery on the opposite wall. To achieve the more elaborate effects and to seat the larger audiences required by "The Frozen Deep," Dickens had to secure additional room. For unknown reasons, he did not consider the simple alternative of renting a small public theater. About the problem of the room, Dickens first consulted T. P. Cooke, a veteran character actor, who offered to secure stable tents and "middle-distance tables." After this consultation, Dickens remarked, "Since then, I have arranged to do it all my own way and with my own carpenter." [65] Dickens specified his "own way": "I have put up a wooden house at the back of the schoolroom (my own architect!) to help the effect, and the stage is 30 feet long." [66] Charles, Jr., explained that the bay was used as part of the stage and that access to the garden addition was gained by removing the bay windows.[67]

Dickens' solution of the room problem is more important than it may seem, for Dickens synthesized the script and the stage,

[65] To John Forster, October 18, 1856, *Letters,* II, 807.
[66] To Miss Coutts, December 9, 1856, *Heart,* p. 331.
[67] "Reminiscences," p. 20.

achieving a harmony that the reviewers regarded as remarkable. In a chatty comment about the stage, Charles, Jr., inadvertently revealed the extent of his father's work.

This arrangement . . . was utilized in the most artful manner by the scene painters, as well as by the author, who in the construction of his play kept the necessities and disqualifications of the peculiarly shaped little stage carefully in view, and quite surprising scenic and dramatic effects were the result.[68]

By "the author," Charles, Jr., meant Collins. Only Dickens, however, could have done what Charles, Jr., attributed to Collins. By October 15, Collins apparently had completed his work on the script, and Dickens apparently solved his stage problem with the script in hand.[69] Therefore, though Charles, Jr., thought of Collins as "the author," Dickens must be credited with the stage directions and dialogue written "with the necessities and disqualifications of the peculiarly shaped little stage carefully in view." While revising the script, Dickens was designing the stage. Only he had the vision and the opportunity to shape the script and to design the stage so that their synthesis helped "the effect."

Dickens also worked closely with the "scene painters." William Telbin painted the sets for Act I—the drawing room scene described in the opening stage directions, with a back drop

---

[68] "Reminiscences," pp. 20–21.

[69] On October 7, Dickens wrote that the play was "nearly finished" (to Mrs. Richard Watson, Letters, II, 803–804). On October 11, he knew the approximate number of lines that Alfred Dickens would have to speak (to Alfred Dickens, Letters, II, 805–806). On October 15, a Wednesday, he asked Mrs. Wills to come the following Monday to a reading of "the Play" (to W. H. Wills, Letters, II, 806). Because Dickens revised all of Mrs. Wills' dialogue, in Act III as well as in Act I, he probably had the script for Act III a few days before the reading on October 20.

displaying a typical English landscape and village church. The back drop hung in the "wooden house" that Dickens had built in the garden. Clarkson Stanfield painted the sets for Acts II and III. The sets for Act II depicted the inside of a wooden hut; the back drop, seen when the door of the hut opened, revealed snow and ice in the midst of which flew a British ensign. The sets for Act III depicted the inside of a cave, its open mouth (the bay window) revealing a back drop with a sea scene and a ship flying the British ensign. Stanfield painted the Act Drop, too; this showed a lighthouse washed by a heavy sea. It was probably, though not certainly, the same drop used in 1855 for "The Lighthouse." Telbin contrived lighting effects for Act I that greatly impressed the reviewers with their naturalness. These were basically a sunset and a moonrise that must have been achieved by using gas lines in the garden addition. Paper "snow" fell in this addition during Act II.

Although the painters contrived the actual effects, they worked to support the general effect that Dickens as manager and as principal actor envisioned.

Nothing could induce Telbin yesterday to explain what he was going to do before Stanfield; and nothing would induce Stanfield to explain what *he* was going to do before Telbin. But they had every inch and curve and line in that bow accurately measured by the carpenters, and each requested to have a drawing of the whole made to scale. Then each said he would make his model in card-board, and see what I "thought of it." I have no doubt the thing will be as well done as it can be.[70]

Dickens apparently relied most heavily on Stanfield, with whom he had consulted as early as July and who planned the spectacle

[70] Dickens to Collins, November 1, 1856, *Letters,* II, 809–810.

for the most important acts. Stanfield had had fifteen years of experience as a scene painter for the Royalty, the Pantheon, the Theatre Royal, and Drury Lane before his success as a marine and landscape painter had earned him election to the Royal Academy and made it possible for him to earn his living by more serious painting. As a personal favor to Dickens, Stanfield once again became a scene painter, one of those to whom Charles, Jr., referred so casually. Although relying heavily on Stanfield, Dickens remained responsible for integrating the scenery with the rest of the spectacle and with the performance.

Dickens attended personally to many minor tasks to ensure that the spectacle would be effective. He had new gas lines installed for complex lighting effects; then he found himself in trouble with the "fire office-surveyor" because of the lines. Unable to settle the trouble through correspondence, he met with the secretary of the fire insurance company.[71] In special rehearsals, he practiced with the "Snowboys."[72] He arranged with Mr. Ireland to borrow "Machinery and Properties" from the Theatre Royal and with Nathan of Titchborne Street for the costumes.[73] When Dickens found that one of Stanfield's scenes required "support," he designed and had built a pair of "wings."[74] He asked Telbin whether he wanted the name of his assistant, Grieve, to appear on the playbills and told him that because the furniture was ornate, "the drugget should have no pattern on it."[75] For the later public performances, Dickens concerned him-

[71] Dickens to Thomas Mitton, December 3, 1856, *Letters,* II, 813.
[72] Dickens to Mark Lemon, December 14, 1856, *Letters,* II, 815–816; Henry Fielding Dickens, *The Recollections of Sir Henry Dickens, K. C.* (London, 1934), p. 6.
[73] *Charles Dickens Rare Print Collection,* ed. Seymour Eaton (Philadelphia, 1900), Part III, No. 2, Playbill for Tuesday, January 6, 1857.
[74] Dickens to William Telbin, December 2, 1856, *Letters,* II, 813.
[75] To Telbin, November 10, 1856, *Letters,* II, 810–811.

self with details as slight as a cracked handbell and the size of the paper snow.[76]

Dickens accepted the offer of Francesco Berger, whom Charles, Jr., had met in Leipzig, to write the overture and some of the incidental pieces and to play the piano during the performances. At the time, Berger was only twenty-two years old and relatively unknown. He apparently made little impression on Dickens, who remarked to Collins, "I wish Berger were a little further. Hogarth says that some of the best people out of the Queen's private band would have been charmed to play for nothing, and would have esteemed it a privilege to take all manner of pains; but that of course they can't be put under the said B." [77] Although Berger did not impress Dickens, Dickens greatly impressed Berger, who, after seventy-five years and a very successful career, retained vivid memories of his brief experience with Dickens. These memories help to explain the zeal that Dickens communicated to the group who were helping him to implement his notion. After the rehearsals, Dickens gave elaborate suppers, which required so much meat that the family butcher came to the house inquiring about the large orders.[78] Berger vividly remembered these suppers:

The very numerous rehearsals which preceded the play he produced at his house were always followed by substantial suppers, which all concerned partook of, seated round the large table in his commodious dining-room. The viands would have delighted the heart of John Browdie, for they included a huge joint of cold roast beef, a tongue, a ham, several cold roast fowls, a few raised pies, tarts and jellies, dozens of bottled Guinness and Bass, and ended with punch brewed by the "manager's" own hands. Punch, in those days, meant

---

[76] Dickens to John Thompson, August 13, 1857, *Letters*, II, 870.
[77] October 15, 1856, *Letters*, II, 806.
[78] Charles Dickens, Jr., "Reminiscences," p. 21.

a deliciously odoured compound of rum and brandy, spice, sugar and lemon-juice, ladled piping hot, into good-sized tumblers from a bowl the size of a small bath.[79]

This description suggests that genuine affection and harmony pervaded the whole group, that Dickens conveyed to those around him some of the cheer which pervades his early novels. It suggests, also, the kind of relief that the mere activity of staging, aside from the "effect" of the performances, provided for Dickens.

In April 1856, Dickens had written in a rather grim tone about the aging Macready's effect on him. In December 1856, burdened with more physical duties than he had had in April, Dickens wrote to Macready in a jovial tone about his "aged friend."

You may faintly imagine, my venerable friend, the occupation of these also gray hairs, between Golden Marys, Little Dorrits, Household Wordses, four stage-carpenters entirely boarding on the premises, a carpenter's shop erected in the back garden, size always boiling over on all the fires, Stanfield perpetually elevated on planks and splashing himself from head to foot, Telbin requiring impossibilities of smart gas men, and a legion of prowling nondescripts for ever shrinking in and out. Calm amidst the wreck, your aged friend glides away on the Dorrit stream, forgetting the uproar for a stretch of hours, refreshing himself with a ten or twelve miles' walk, pitches headforemost into foaming rehearsals, placidly emerges for editorial

[79] Francesco Berger, 97 (London, 1931), p. 17. The publisher's note, p. vii, states that Berger published over two hundred solos and songs, served for twenty-five years as Professor of Piano-Forte at the Royal Academy of Music, for forty-five as Professor of Piano-Forte at the Guildhall School of Music, and for twenty-seven as the Honorable Secretary of the Royal Philharmonic Society.

purposes, smokes over buckets of distemper with Mr. Stanfield aforesaid, again calmly floats upon the Dorrit waters.[80]

Dickens mentioned his "gray hairs" and called himself "aged,"
but he treated age as a joke. There was chaos all around him and
others were upset, but he, despite his tremendous expenditure of
energy, was placid and calm. He apparently was pleased by the
progress of the staging and expected Macready to understand
and to appreciate the growth of a play and its manager's efforts.
With opening night less than a month away and the audience
already invited, Dickens would not have found the chaos a joke
if he had doubted his ability to bring order from it. He was
enjoying the demands on his energy and anticipating a trium-
phant conclusion to his multiple activities.

Dickens had begun to draw up a formal guest list and to send
out invitations as early as October 10, because he wanted to
secure as guests people who would have many demands on their
time during the Christmas season.[81] Some received an announce-
ment of the play accompanied by a playbill; others received
personal letters from Dickens. To the Duke of Devonshire,
Dickens wrote:

The moment the first bill is printed for the first night of the New
Play I told you of, I send it to you, in the hope that you will grace it
with your presence. There is not one of the old actors whom you will
fail to inspire as no one else can. And I hope you will see a little
result of a friendly union of the Arts, that you may think worth
seeing, and that you can see nowhere else. . . . I shall hope for the
first, unless you dash me.[82]

[80] December 13, 1856, *Letters*, II, 815.
[81] Dickens to Mr. and Mrs. Cowden Clarke, October 10, 1856, *Letters*,
II, 805; Dickens to William Telbin, November 10, 1856, *Letters*, II,
810–811.
[82] December 1, 1856, *Letters*, II, 812–813.

Dickens usually wrote in a less deferential tone than this, but in some letters he displayed a similar anxiety to have particular persons present, even Miss Coutts' companion, Mrs. Brown, whom he disliked.[83] (A facsimile of the playbill appears on page 7.)

Besides seeking a select audience, Dickens also sought publicity, an unusual action for any manager of an amateur production in a private home. He encouraged three important reviewers to comment freely on the performances—John Oxenford, Dramatic Critic for *The Times;* George Hogarth, Musical and Dramatic Critic for *The Illustrated London News;* and David Hastings, Musical Critic for the *Morning Herald.* To Hastings, Dickens explained:

I ought to let you know that I don't wish to coquet about next Tuesday's play, and that if you should think it of any public interest or merit I beg you to use your own free discretion as to noticing it; not being restrained by the supposition that any privacy on that head is implied in the invitation. I have written both to Oxenford and to Hogarth (who will also be here on the first night) exactly to this effect, by this same post. The Play will be seen by so many people of various conditions, that I feel it would be an affectation in me to make a mystery of it—while it would be hardly fair, moreover, to the other public men who have taken pains with it.[84]

That such an explanation was necessary if the play was to receive publicity is made clear by the reviewer for *The Athenaeum,* who had received an invitation but no accompanying explanation. After briefly and genteelly commenting on the performance, this reviewer scolded his colleagues like Hastings and Oxenford for what seemed bad manners: "We may express generally—we hope without breach of good manners—our

[83] To Miss Coutts, December 9, 1856, *Heart,* pp. 330–331.
[84] December 30, 1856, *Letters,* II, 819–820.

pleasure in the play and in its performance; but we do not feel ourselves free, like some of our literary brethren, to enter into details and criticism of a private entertainment." [85] Only after the public performances in July did this reviewer, with some relief, write, "We are now justified in discontinuing the reticence with which we have hitherto treated Mr. Wilkie Collins's play"; [86] he commented extensively and enthusiastically on the acting and the scenic effects.

Dickens' reasons for seeking publicity are not clear. He had not sought to publicize any previous Twelfth Night production. In 1857, he was not planning more than four performances and was not afraid that he would have empty seats for these. By December 3, he knew that "the Lord Chief Justice, the Chief Baron, and half the Bench were coming." [87] Before opening night, he had to refuse late requests for invitations, even from members of the company for their friends. Collins and Berger were the only "public men" who might really benefit from a successful production, though several public men would have lost some of their reputation if the effect in 1857 had been like that in 1866. Dickens expected, or at least hoped, that the strong effect which he anticipated would interest the general public as well as his friends. His earlier letters to Miss Coutts, the Duke of Devonshire, and W. C. Macready had already implied this. He may have hoped that large numbers of people would share his faith in the nature of man, his faith in the power of the noble sentiments, which the action of "The Frozen Deep" affirms. He may have hoped that the play would stimulate interest in the new expedition to search for Franklin, which was being organized at the time of the performances and which was supported

---

[85] January 10, 1857, p. 56.
[86] July 18, 1857, p. 916.
[87] Dickens to Thomas Mitton, December 3, 1856, *Letters*, II, 813.

by articles in *Household Words*. One can be certain only that Dickens had a highly unusual desire to publicize an amateur theatrical.

The play opened unofficially on Monday, January 5, 1857, before an audience of servants, tradespeople, and their friends. This performance served as a dress rehearsal for the semipublic performances which began on January 6 and were repeated on January 8, 12, and 14. Approximately ninety persons came to each performance. Among the guests were Rev. Henry Hart Milman, Dean of St. Paul's; Rev. Edward Tagart, a Unitarian preacher whose sermons Dickens liked; Miss Coutts; Edward Marjoribanks, a partner in Coutts and Company; W. C. Macready; Sir James Emerson Tennent, a member of Parliament who had supported the Reform Bill of 1832 and the repeal of the Corn Laws and to whom Dickens later dedicated *Our Mutual Friend;* Sir Charles Eastlake, President of the Royal Academy and Director of the National Gallery; Sir John Campbell, Lord Chief Justice; Sir Jonathan Frederick Pollock, Lord Chief Baron; Sir George Bramwell, Judge of the Exchequer; Sir James Shaw Willes, Judge of Common Pleas; and Sir Alexander Cockburn, Chief Justice of Common Pleas.[88]

Dickens was satisfied with the effect of the performances. To Mrs. Brown, he wrote:

I am delighted to hear that Mr. Marjoribanks was so much pleased by the Play. Its effect on the three other audiences we have had, has been the same; and I certainly have never seen people so strongly

[88] No guest list was published. For sources, see Dickens to Milman, January 9, 1857, *Letters*, II, 825; to Tagart, January 20, 1857, *Letters,* II, 829; to Mrs. Brown, January 2, 1857, *Heart*, pp. 332–333; to Wills, January 7, 1857, *Letters*, II, 824; to Tennent, January 9, 1857, *Letters,* II, 824–825; Sir Charles Eastlake to Wilkie Collins, January 10, 1857 (M.A. 81).

affected by theatrical means. To-night is our closing night. By an absurd coincidence three fourths of the Judges I know, preferred this night to another. . . . Cockburn, the new Chief Justice of the Common Pleas, rather spoils the effect of the absurdity in having been here on Monday. He wouldn't go after the Play, but would come and make speeches at the Green Room Supper. I never saw anything better of its kind than the genuine and hearty way in which, without the least affectation, he shewed his pleasure.[89]

The professional reviewers, also, observed that the performances had made an unusually strong impression on the select audience. They lauded the performances and informed the public about their effect, thus making the private theatricals the public event that Dickens had hoped they would become.

The performance on January 14 ended all the activity that Dickens had planned originally for "The Frozen Deep." He continued to write enthusiastically about the play's having been "the most complete thing" anyone had ever seen and about its unusual effect on the audience. But on January 28, he wrote to Macready, "The theatre has disappeared, the house is restored to its usual conditions of order, the family are tranquil and domestic, dove-eyed peace is enthroned in this study, fire-eyed radicalism in its master's breast." [90] Dickens assumed that the performances of "The Frozen Deep" had ended; then he heard unexpected rumors that he might be asked to bring the play before Queen Victoria. Excitedly, he wrote to Miss Coutts, "The wildest legends are circulating about town, to the effect that the Queen proposes to have The Frozen Deep at Windsor. I have heard nothing of it otherwise, but slink about holding my breath." [91] The anxiously awaited proposal never came. The expectations the rumors aroused, however, perhaps had some-

[89] January 14, 1857, *Heart*, pp. 333–334.
[90] *Letters*, II, 831.   [91] February 3, 1857, *Heart*, p. 336.

thing to do with subsequent events that resulted in a performance before the Queen and six performances before audiences
who paid for their tickets.

On June 10, Dickens learned that Douglas Jerrold, an old
acquaintance, had died the previous day.[92] For his widow and
unmarried daughter, Dickens planned a series of benefits, which
would include performances of "The Frozen Deep." He evidently hoped from the first to perform before Queen Victoria,
for on June 12 he informed Collins, "I am trying for the
queen." [93] Dickens told the complete story of his successful attempts to Miss Coutts.[94] Although knowing that the Queen
would refuse to support a benefit for an individual, Dickens
approached Colonel C. B. Phipps, Equerry to Queen Victoria,
and asked if the Queen would support the Jerrold benefits by
coming to one of the performances of "The Frozen Deep,"
which Dickens had decided to give at the Gallery of Illustration.[95] When the request elicited the expected refusal, Dickens
again called on Colonel Phipps and was informed that although
the Queen could not support the benefit, she would like to see
the play, and would be willing to invite Dickens to produce it at
Buckingham Palace. Dickens replied that if the performance
could not be given otherwise, he would bring the play to the

[92] Dickens to John Forster, June 10, 1857, *Letters*, II, 854.
[93] M.A. 81.
[94] June 20, 1857, *Heart*, pp. 341–342.
[95] Henry Fielding Dickens noted that the ordinary entertainment by
Mr. and Mrs. Thomas German Reed, songs and impersonations, was "a
great attraction to the public, not only to ordinary playgoers, but to others
whose religious views kept them away from the regular theatres" (*Recollections*, pp. 315–316). Edgar Browne described the Gallery of Illustration as having "a regular stage on a very small scale but exactly like the
real thing, with footlights, a curtain, and costumes" (*Phiz and Dickens*
[New York, 1914], p. 140).

Palace. Since he would not feel easy about the social position of his daughters under such circumstances, however, he asked that the Queen consider coming to a strictly private performance at the Gallery of Illustration, to be held a week before the benefit performances. To this counterproposal, the Queen agreed.[96]

Dickens arranged the private performance for July 4 and in addition to the Royal Party invited a few members of his family and such acquaintances as Thackeray and Hans Christian Andersen.[97] The Royal Party included Queen Victoria, Prince Albert, King Leopold of Belgium, Prince Frederick William of Prussia (recently engaged to Princess Victoria), and various members of the Royal family and attendants.[98] About the response of such spectators, Dickens apparently had misgivings,

[96] In *The Speeches of Charles Dickens* (Oxford, 1960), pp. 373–374, K. J. Fielding accepts a different version. Rumors in 1857 reported Jerrold's son angered by the benefits, Dickens' doing the whole thing out of vanity, and the Queen's seeking out Dickens (see the article from the *Inverness Courier* reprinted in *The Weekly Chronicle and Register*, July 4, 1857, p. 3). They were rebutted by an article in *The Athenaeum*, July 4, 1857, p. 854. In a letter to Miss Henriette Wulff on July 19, 1857, Andersen called them "abominable"; in a letter to the Grand Duke of Sachse-Weimar on October 30, 1857, he attacked Jerrold's son as "ungrateful" (Bredsdorff, *Andersen and Dickens*, pp. 106, 131). Fielding accepts the story that Dickens allegedly told to Mrs. James T. Fields during his last American tour (see M. A. de Wolfe Howe, *Memories of a Hostess: A Chronicle of Eminent Friendships Drawn Chiefly from the Diaries of Mrs. James T. Fields* [London, 1923], pp. 188–190).

[97] Andersen, in his diary and letters for this period, described the floral decorations and his experiences during the performances and parties for the cast. See his diary entry for July 4, 1857, his letter to Miss Henriette Wulff, July 6, 1857, and his letter to the Queen Dowager of Denmark, July 14, 1857 (Bredsdorff, *Andersen and Dickens*, pp. 79–80, 101, 104). Bredsdorff printed on p. 81 a facsimile of the July 4 playbill and facing p. 96 a photograph of the amateur company.

[98] *The Times*, July 6, 1857, p. 8.

for he wrote to Collins, "There is a great deal at stake, and it *must be* well done." [99] Their response must have allayed his fears and delighted him. Georgina Hogarth reported, "The Queen and her party made a most excellent audience—so far from being cold, as we expected, they cried and laughed, and applauded and made as much demonstration as so small a party (they were not more than fifty) could do." [100] After creating such a successful effect, Dickens risked spoiling the whole evening. Wanting to thank Dickens personally for the pleasure he had given her, the Queen sent for him after the last act of "The Frozen Deep." Before her messenger reached him, he had changed into comic dress for the farce, which was to follow, and he bluntly refused her first and then her repeated request to appear before her, excusing himself because of his costume.

The Queen must have been amused rather than angered by Dickens' refusal, because the next day she instructed Colonel Phipps to write Dickens a letter thanking him for the pleasure he had given her and expressing her admiration of his acting and of the play. Out of politeness, Colonal Phipps said that he could not repeat all the praise he had heard of Dickens' acting, but that he could tell Dickens about the Queen's admiration of Mark Lemon's and the ladies' acting and particularly of the "piece itself."

There was every temptation to an author to increase the effect of the play by representing the triumph of the evil passions, but it was particularly pleasing to Her Majesty to find a much higher lesson taught in the victory of the better and nobler feelings and of the

---

[99] June 26, 1857, *Letters*, II, 858.
[100] To Mrs. Winter, July 21, 1857, *The Love Romance of Charles Dickens: Told in His Letters to Maria Beadnell (Mrs. Winter)*, ed. Walter Dexter (London, 1936), p. 106.

reward—the only one he could obtain—to Richard, in his self content before his death.[101]

Colonel Phipps began his letter by informing Dickens that he had "hardly ever seen her Majesty and HRH so much pleased" and ended by saying, "*Unofficially* I may tell you that everything went off as well as possible."

Dickens produced the public performances on July 11, 18, and 25. Although he set a relatively high price on the tickets (stalls one guinea, area seats ten shillings and sixpence, amphitheatre seats five shillings), by July 4 all the seats for the first two performances had been sold.[102] The reviewers for *The Times* and for *The Spectator* noted that with an audience that had paid "liberally" for the privilege of watching the performances, the amateurs faced a more difficult situation than they had faced with the invited audiences at Tavistock House. Both reviewers cited the striking success with the public audiences as evidence of the quality of the performances.[103] John Oxenford asserted that such an audience was difficult to please, but that their deep and genuine admiration was shown when, as the curtain descended, "there was literally a gasp of applause."[104] The reviewer for *The Leader* judged the performance remarkable for the "purity of its tone" and for "its power over the laughter, the tears, and the interest of the audience."[105] Even the reviewer for *The Saturday Review*, who qualified his praise by noting that "there is much in dramatic art which is of a higher kind," asserted that the amateurs had surpassed profes-

[101] C. B. Phipps to Charles Dickens, July 5, 1857, M.A. 81.

[102] *The Athenaeum*, July 4, 1857, p. 854.

[103] *The Times*, July 13, 1857, p. 12; *The Spectator*, July 18, 1857, p. 751.

[104] *The Times*, July 13, 1857, p. 12.

[105] *The Leader*, July 18, 1857, p. 692.

sionals, there being "nothing to be seen at present on the English stage which equals the Frozen Deep." [106]

After the first of these public performances on July 11, Dickens was approached by John Deane, manager of the Great Manchester Art Exhibition. Deane asked Dickens to give performances of "The Frozen Deep" in the New Free Trade Hall, assuring him that each benefit performance there would raise at least £700. Dickens refused. First, he was afraid that in the large theater "the great delicacy and completeness" of his sets could not be seen by the audiences. Second, he was certain that his amateur actresses could not project their voices well enough to be heard by a large crowd. Deane persisted. When Dickens discovered that despite filled theaters for all the Gallery of Illustration performances he would not raise the £2,000 promised Mrs. Jerrold and her daughter, he agreed to examine the Manchester theater. After his trip to Manchester, he decided to risk giving two performances there. He said nothing more about the sets after this trip, but he announced that he had decided to replace his amateur actresses with professionals, the best he could find available. He cast Mrs. Ternan as Nurse Esther, Maria Ternan as Clara Burnham, Ellen Ternan as Lucy Crayford, Ellen Sabine as Rose Ebsworth, and Mrs. George Vining as Mrs. Steventon. The impending death of Frederick Evans' grandmother necessitated one change among the minor actors— Charles Collins, younger brother of Wilkie, replaced Evans as Darker.[107]

---

[106] *The Saturday Review*, August 1, 1857, pp. 106–107.

[107] These details may be found in Dickens' letters (*Letters,* II) to John Deane, July 12, 1857, pp. 861–862; to W. C. Macready, July 13, 1857, p. 862; to Collins, August 2, 1857, p. 866; to Mrs. Compton, August 2, 1857, pp. 866–867; to Collins, August 17, 1857, p. 871. See also the playbill that Collins printed with *The Frozen Deep*, p. 6.

Apparently the sets lost some of their effectiveness in the Free Trade Hall, for Charles, Jr., remarked, "Our little fit-up looked not much bigger than a Punch and Judy show." [108] But this loss did not prevent Dickens from achieving his greatest popular success at Manchester with the play. Two thousand people bought tickets for each of the scheduled performances on Friday, August 21, and Saturday, August 22.[109] Because many more wanted to see the play than could buy tickets for these two performances, Dickens gave an unscheduled third performance on August 24, a Monday, when he did not have the benefit of the week-end crowds attracted by the Art Treasures Exhibition.[110] Despite his remark about Punch-and-Judy-size scenery, Charles, Jr., judged that "the play went quite as well as it had ever done in the Tavistock House schoolroom." [111] Collins asserted that these performances were "the finest of all the representations of 'The Frozen Deep.'" [112] Dickens was jubilant, describing his success as "enormous." [113] He ended his public connection with the play by publishing a letter, signed also by Arthur Smith, Secretary of the Jerrold Fund, announcing that

[108] "Reminiscences," p. 22. For the history and description of the Free Trade Hall see the report of the opening ceremonies in *The Times,* October 8, 1856, p. 5, and October 10, 1856, p. 10. There is a facsimile of a watercolor drawing of the Manchester theater and a scene from Act II in *The Dickensian,* LIV (1958), 130.

[109] Dickens to Miss Coutts, September 5, 1857, *Letters,* II, 876–877.

[110] Berger, 97, p. 16. A facsimile playbill for the August 24 performance is printed in *The Dickensian,* LIV (1958), 164.

[111] "Reminiscences," p. 22.

[112] *The Frozen Deep,* p. 4. Collins made several curious errors in his remarks, saying that after the Gallery of Illustration performances, productions were put on in "some of the principal towns in England," that the play was performed only twice at Manchester, and that each audience had numbered three thousand.

[113] To Mrs. Owen, September 2, 1857, *Letters,* II, 876.

after the payment of all expenses a clear profit of £2,000 had been raised for Mrs. Jerrold and her daughter.[114]

These Manchester performances brought to an exciting and successful climax Dickens' activity as a producer of, and actor in, amateur theatricals. They were the last of a series of calculated risks that Dickens undertook in 1857 by bringing a minor romantic drama and an amateur cast from the shelter of the private theater in Tavistock House. Each of the risks brought Dickens successively greater returns of public esteem and spread "the effect" wider than he could have anticipated. The effect was felt so strongly and by so many different kinds of people that a modern reader of the script is likely to find the responses of the audiences incredible. The nature of this effect and the significance of the success have yet to be examined.

[114] *The Leader,* September 5, 1857, p. 860.

The Effect

The audiences experienced the climactic effect of the performances as pathos. Dickens had anticipated this effect as early as July 1856, when he had remarked that he would take "intense" satisfaction from making the Duke of Devonshire "wretched." In September 1857, he informed Miss Coutts that he had been "very excited by the crying of two thousand people over the grave of Richard Wardour." Then, in detail, he described how Maria Ternan had set the whole cast to weeping. As she knelt over the dying Wardour, her face had had a "natural emotion in it," and she had wept uncontrollably, the tears streaming "out of her eyes into his mouth, down his beard, all over his rags." She had begged Dickens not to die on stage. Watching her, Mark Lemon, "the softest hearted of men," had begun to cry in sympathy and by the time the curtain fell, everyone on stage had been crying. Dickens had never seen "anything more prettily simple and unaffected," and judged that Maria Ternan "had one of the most genuine and feeling hearts in the world." [115] The event impressed Dickens so much that three months later he repeated the story to Mrs. Richard Watson, introducing it with the remark:

All last summer I had a transitory satisfaction in rending the very heart out of my body by doing that Richard Wardour part. It was a good thing to have a couple of thousand people all rigid and frozen together, in the palm of one's hand—as at Manchester—and to see the hardened Carpenters at the sides crying and trembling at it night after night.[116]

[115] September 5, 1857, *Letters*, II, 876–877.
[116] December 7, 1857, *The Dickensian*, XXXVIII (1942), 189–191.

The tears were apparently more numerous at Manchester than they had been earlier; Dickens had mentioned several times that his audiences had been "strongly affected," but had not remarked on any event comparable to that at Manchester. Others, though, had noted tears and the pathos of which they were the sign as the climactic effect of all the performances.[117]

This effect depended in part on the presence of unusually sympathetic audiences. Reviewers noted that the Tavistock House audiences had been comprised of "the highest celebrities in law, literature, art, and fashion." [118] They did not note that most of these "celebrities" were Dickens' acquaintances or friends, who watched the play performed during the Christmas season in his home, to which they had come as guests. When Queen Victoria and her party, also as guests, watched the performance, they knew what the response of "the highest celebrities" had been. The responses of the "celebrities" and of the aristocracy had been widely publicized before anyone with a ticket watched a performance, and those buying tickets knew that their money would help support a widow and an unmarried daughter. Finally, the Manchester audiences had had opportunities to read about the enthusiasm of all the London audiences. Unless the mid-Victorians were much freer from the compulsion to conform than their modern counterparts, there must have been a cumulative band-wagon development to help make the Manchester performances "the finest of all the representations."

Neither the audiences' sympathy nor the pressure to conform would have made the performances successful, however, if Dickens had not achieved a high quality of melodramatic production.

[117] For examples see *The Examiner*, January 17, 1857, p. 38; Bredsdorff, *Andersen and Dickens*, p. 79 (Andersen's diary entry for July 4, 1857); *The Illustrated London News*, July 18, 1857, p. 59.
[118] *The Times*, January 7, 1857, p. 7.

Macready, an old friend of Dickens but also an experienced professional manager and actor, was strongly affected by the quality of the performance. To Lady Pollock, he commented, "It was remarkably, extraordinarily clever, in all respects; I mean positively so, and rendered so much more effective by the general harmony of the party. I do not wonder at your having recourse to your cambric. The performance excited me very much." [119] The cleverness and harmony caught the attention of all the reviewers, who found the spectacle and acting unusually fresh and natural, in contrast to the spectacle and acting of the professional stage. They had been accustomed, apparently, to seeing rather conventional sets and costumes and to hearing affected tones.[120] They were impressed by the "natural" quality of the new spectacle, by the "charm" of hearing ladies on the stage speak like ladies, and by the fervid power of Dickens' acting. Some reviewers thought that Dickens' acting "might teach professionals much that they were willfully ignorant of" and that it "might open a new era for the stage." [121] All of them wrote as though Dickens had had no professional tradition from which to copy the kind of realism in spectacle and manner that he had achieved as manager. They regarded him as an innovator and attributed the success of the performances primarily to his innovations.

[119] *Macready's Reminiscences and Selections from His Diaries and Letters,* ed. Sir Frederick Pollock (2 vols.; London, 1875), II, 409.

[120] Allardyce Nicoll describes a general movement during the first part of the nineteenth century toward more realistic spectacle and more restrained acting, climaxed in 1865 with the production of Tom Robertson's *Society (The English Theatre* [London, 1936], pp. 144–172). Reviewers did not comment on "The Frozen Deep" as part of a general movement.

[121] *The Athenaeum,* July 18, 1857, p. 916; *The Leader,* January 10, 1857, p. 45.

Dickens had deliberately sought the support of realistic spectacle. He proudly referred to the completeness of the play, thinking of his historically accurate properties and scenery and recognizing that he had surpassed professional managers:

> I believe that anything so complete has never been seen. We had an act at the North Pole, where the slightest and greatest thing the eye beheld were equally taken from the books of the Polar voyagers. Out of thirty people, there were certainly not two who might not have gone straight to the North Pole itself, completely furnished for the winter! [122]

To attain this completeness, Dickens had revised much in Collins' draft, substituting, for instance, a cask for Collins' table—an object which the explorers did not carry on their sledges when they abandoned their ships—and a hammock for the wooden "bed place" that Collins had assigned to John Want. The explorers carried planks with them to build shelters, using a few of these to build wooden "berths" for the officers. The common seamen, like John Want, slept in hammocks. Dickens also accepted Stanfield's suggestion that a piece of rock be substituted for a chair in Act III as "clearly an improvement." [123] These, of course, were among the "slightest" things; the principal "natural" effect depended upon the scenery and the lighting.

This spectacle, especially when viewed in a small theater, helped the audiences to feel as though they were participating in a credible stage action.

The scenery is wonderfully good on its tiny scale. After a prologue delivered from behind a curtain in the rich voice, and with the fine elocution of Mr. Forster, we find ourselves first in the pretty drawing-room of a country house, having one of those sweet picturesque

[122] To W. F. De Cerjat, January 17, 1857, *Letters*, II, 827.
[123] Dickens to Collins, November 1, 1856, *Letters*, II, 809-810.

views so thoroughly English, with a village church and spire in the distance, standing out in relief against the strong red lights of a fine sunset. As the light fades with the advancing evening a grey tone comes over the landscape with the most natural effect. This scene is painted by Mr. Telbin. We are next shivering in a hut in the Arctic regions, all bare, dreary, and grim. As the door opens and admits the cutting blasts we see the falling snow and the far-spreading frozen waste. In this scene of desolation there is one warm, vivid colour, speaking of home and hope. It is the British ensign, blowing out straight and bold in the icy breeze, as much to say, "Where am I not? And where I am aloft, who despairs? who has not heart and hope and resolution?"

We are next and last in a cave on the coast of Newfoundland, with a Queen's ship anchored in the offing, about to sail home with the rescued voyagers. These two latter scenes are by the masterly hand of Stanfield. Who else, indeed, could paint such a sea? [124]

This description emphasizes stock responses to the "thoroughly English" view, the "frozen waste," and the "British ensign," also flown on the "Queen's ship" and visible throughout Act III, though the reviewer did not mention it. The reviewer responded strongly to the general situation of British seamen in peril and apparently expected his readers to sympathize with his response. The British ensign symbolized "home and hope," qualities of courage and resolution embodied in the tradition of the British

---

[124] *The Examiner*, January 17, 1857, pp. 38–39. Oxenford described the curtain hiding Forster as a "dense gauze," which gave the effect of "dispersing mists" as it was raised (*The Times*, January 7, 1857, p. 7). Dickens later changed minor details. In the Gallery of Illustration performances, Dickens delivered the Prologue and had a gun fired from the back cloth as Act III ended (Bredsdorff, *Andersen and Dickens*, p. 79). On the larger stage at Manchester, he had a small boat drawn toward the cave entrance as Act III ended. This is shown by an addition to the stage directions in his handwriting. He may have made other changes in the spectacle—for example, have had a flag raised—but there is no clear evidence that he did.

gentleman. The symbol implies a faith in the nature of the men like that to which Dickens had appealed in his Franklin articles. Such stock responses to the scenery would have supported the major dramatic action, encouraging the viewers to associate the actors with traditional heroes, in particular, of course, the Arctic explorers.

Another reviewer was untypically impressed more strongly by the realistic lighting effects in Act I than he was by the scenery. His description of the scene in which Nurse Esther began to prophesy reveals the impact that these effects could make.

The warm red hues of the west pale into the grey and spectral moonshine (an effect marvellously contrived by Mr. Telbin). She stands in the gathering gloom, darkly relieved against the misty blue of the window, and, in a voice half frightened, half denunciatory, tells them of a vision of blood which passes before her eyes from the Northern seas. Lucy Crayford, shuddering with dread, calls for lights; Clara Burnham falls senseless; and the first act is concluded.

Of the effect of this scene, from the commencement to the end, it would be difficult to convey an adequate idea. The weary, lonely grief of the four companions; the spirit of quiet, gentle sorrow that moves over the whole performance; the sweet, sad melody sung by two of the young ladies in the inner room, while Clara is telling her story to Lucy; the awful forebodings of the Scotch nurse; the deep, yet melancholy sympathy of the evening light and the solemn stealing in of the white moonrise; the wretchedness and the terror of the ladies, and the shuddering awe of Esther's vision (not raved out, according to transmitted fashion, but all quiet and intense)—these elements contribute to a general effect which is new to our stage, because based on Nature instead of on tradition.[125]

Even after Dickens modified the use of Nurse Esther's second sight, it could appear to be a preternatural power. Although accepting it as a credible power of vision, the reviewer still

[125] *The Leader*, January 10, 1857, pp. 44–45.

asserted that the "general effect" was "based on Nature." By this last phrase, he apparently meant only that the lighting was more realistic and the acting more restrained than he had been accustomed to seeing. Because the lighting and acting seemed "natural," he accepted the "vision of blood" as being included within a "general effect," the whole of which was "natural." His description conveys, implicitly, an idea of how much the more credible events in Acts II and III may have benefited from the spectacle.

The more typical reviewers admired the novel charm of the actresses, but recognized their performance as merely effective preparation for the subsequent action. They acknowledged the charm in terms like these:

> We may venture to express the pleasure with which we listened to the conversation of a stage drawing-room, pronounced with the accent and tone of a real drawing-room. Everyone accustomed to professional theatricals must, on this occasion, have felt how novel a charm it was to hear the ladies of a play talk like ladies.[126]

In summarizing the action, reviewers clearly indicated the subordinate function of these ladies.

> Under the title of "The Frozen Deep," the rigours of the Arctic regions are scenically portrayed, both by description and the pencil of Mr. Stanfield and Mr. Danson. Previously, however, to their exhibition, we have a most effective domestic scene in Kent, painted by Mr. Telbin, in which the members of the family of Captain Ebsworth and Lieutenants Crayford and Steventon, who are on board certain vessels engaged in an expedition at the North Pole, are assembled, and disclose the sufferings and suspense by which they are agonized during the absence of their beloved relatives. . . . Clara's fears are awakened, and haunt her imagination continually. To deepen the impression still more, Nurse Esther pretends to

[126] *The Saturday Review*, August 1, 1857, p. 107.

second sight, and predicts the most fatal catastrophe; this character was admirably impersonated by her representative. The Arctic scenes are, however, the great scenes of this excellent drama.[127]

Although charming in itself, the natural manner of speaking and behaving was worth notice principally because it made credible the women's concern for the men missing from their families. In the context of the comfortable drawing-room and the thoroughly English view, the women won a strong interest in, and sympathy for, the men, who were to appear "shivering in a hut in the Arctic regions, all bare, dreary, and grim."

Among these men, the reviewers attended little to the father, husband, brother, or sweetheart, largely because these roles were strictly subordinated to Wardour's. Mark Lemon, as a hearty naval officer and Wardour's only friend, was praised in most of the reviews. Augustus Egg, as the humorous cook, was praised in a few. Except for Dickens, the other actors were virtually ignored. Dickens, as the potential villain and as the ultimate hero, drew almost all of the reviewers' attention. They commented extensively on his performance, crediting it with the impact that produced fear in Act II and pathos at the end of Act III. In part, Dickens impressed them because, like the ladies, he avoided affected tones and gestures, speaking and behaving as any British gentleman with strong passions might have spoken and behaved under similar stresses. Partly because of this manner, Dickens' performance seemed "true" or "natural." It seemed "true" in some larger sense, however. Through Wardour, Dickens revealed his own "intense sympathy with humanity" and subtly identified "the individual man with the breadth and depth of our general nature." [128] In his strangely powerful and creative performance, Dickens gave Wardour's inner life a dimension

[127] *The Illustrated London News*, January 17, 1857, p. 51.
[128] *The Leader*, January 10, 1857, p. 45.

and credibility that neither he nor his reviewers could fully explain.

Few reviewers qualified their praise of Dickens' performance. Among those who did, one noted that because the play was "melodramatic," there was "much in dramatic art of a higher kind," and therefore he could not judge "at what point Mr. Dickens's powers might fail him." This reviewer then observed that the play was superior to anything on the professional stage, attributing its superiority chiefly to Dickens' acting.

His acting is quiet, strong, natural, and effective. It appeals to the imagination of the audience; it seems to convey more than the expressions or the situations can account for, and yet is free from exaggeration; it is a work of art, but the art is concealed; it is the studied embodiment of a conception, and yet appears the simple exhibition of a real character.

                    .   .   .   .   .

There is much that is effective in the author's conception of Wardour; but unquestionably the part derives its chief interest from the way in which it is rendered by Mr. Dickens. The sullen bluntness, and the utter recklessness to his own fate, with which Wardour is first seen mixing among his companions—the burst of wonder, madness, and jealousy with which he discovers the secret of the carving—the irony with which he wards off the good advice bestowed on him by the friendly captain [sic]—are all alike telling and admirable. The dying scene in the last act requires even still greater powers, for the whole feeling has to be wrought up to a high level; and yet the slightest overstraining, the least excess of sentimentalism, would make the scene insufferably unreal and absurd. To see it acted as Mr. Dickens acts it shows what a genius for the art can achieve.[129]

This reviewer judged that Dickens had transcended the limitations of the script. Richard Wardour was "the studied embodi-

[129] *The Saturday Review*, August 1, 1857, pp. 106–107.

ment of a conception," which somehow conveyed more than the dialogue or the situations could explain. Dickens had done more than merely implement the "author's conception"; by means of an "art" which was concealed, he had given a new dimension to this conception, appealing to the imagination of the audience so that he succeeded in bringing the feeling up to a "high level" without falling into bathos, which the reviewer recognized as clearly a danger. The reviewer conceded Dickens' success, but like most of his colleagues did not attempt to explain it.

One reviewer devoted most of his review to explaining the concealed "art." When John Oxenford had reviewed a Tavistock House performance, he had commented generally, like the other reviewers, on what he had seen, mentioning the high quality of the spectacle and of the subordinate acting, summarizing the action, and noting the strange power of Dickens' acting. In his later review of a Gallery of Illustration performance, Oxenford discussed little except Dickens' acting, trying to explain its appeal. His review is particularly valuable because immediately after the performance, he had talked at length with men who were " 'up to everything,' especially in matters connected with public amusement." Their conversation had consisted of "a laudatory criticism of detail." Because Oxenford had the advantage of this conversation as well as of his own experience with at least two performances, he seems the best contemporary authority on Dickens' "art" in "The Frozen Deep."

The performance of Mr. Dickens as the vindictive and (afterwards) penitent Richard Wardour is, in the truest sense of the word, a creation. Nay, we may go further and say that it is the creation of a literary man—that it is doubtful whether any mere actor, unless under the influence of some extraordinary sympathy with the part assumed, would attempt to fill up an outline with that elaborate detail that is introduced by Mr. Dickens into Mr. Collins's sketch.

We feel that if Mr. Dickens had had to describe in narrative form the situations of the *Frozen Deep*, instead of acting them, he would have covered whole pages in recording those manifestations of emotion, which, not having his pen in hand, he now makes by the minutest variations of voice and gesture. Where an ordinary artist would look for "points" of effect he looks for "points" of truth. A specimen of humanity in which every twitch of every muscle can be accounted for is to be presented with all the elaboration of actual nature, no matter whether it be admired or not. When Richard Wardour tells the story of his disappointment in love there is ample opportunity for much noisy grief and many a stride to the footlights, but Mr. Dickens dares to keep down his voice through the whole of the narrative. The effect may be monotonous—but what of that? He who talks not for the sake of display, but simply that he may relieve his mind from an oppressive and almost humiliating burden, will necessarily be monotonous. A man louder under the sense of wrong would have excited less uneasiness in his confidant. But such a man as Mr. Dickens presents—a man strong in the command of his voice, but weak in suppressing the language of his eyes and facial muscles, a man whose constant attempts to hide the internal storm by slight simulations of good fellowship only renders more conspicuous the vastness of that which he would conceal—a man who has a habit of losing his temper in a manner that mere external circumstances do not warrant—such a man is a just object of terror. Richard Wardour, as depicted by Mr. Dickens in the second act of the *Frozen Deep*, is the most perfect representation of dogged vindictiveness that the imagination could conceive.[130]

Oxenford continued with a more general description of Act III, remarking on its "web of emotion," which was so intricate that verbal description could merely indicate the various threads. Much of the description is of the last scenes, in which Richard "is compelled to reveal the generosity of his soul through all the impediments of a mental fog."

[130] *The Times*, July 13, 1857, p. 12.

As understood by Oxenford, Dickens' "art" depended on the extraordinary mobility of Dickens' features, the inflections of his voice, and the gestures of his hand. These means enabled Dickens to embody his creative imagination in his own person and thus to fill out, as no "mere" actor could, the "sketch" or "outline" contained in the script. At the end of Act II, the apparent effect of this embodiment was to implement the suggestions that Dickens had given the audience in the Prologue. "Vastness" and "internal storm" imply that Oxenford felt as though Wardour contained within him the "'vast Profound'" mentioned in the Prologue.

Collins himself apparently felt that Dickens had transcended the limitations of the "sketch" in the script. Despite his part in the conception of Wardour, Collins was "terrified" near the end of Act III when Dickens lunged at him in the wings to carry him into the cave. Collins "always shook like a mould of jelly, and muttered, 'This is an awful thing!' " [131]

Finally, Dickens thought of his performance as manager and actor as being creative. In thanking Sir James Tennent for his compliments, Dickens explained what the play as a whole had meant to him.

As to the play itself; when it is made as good as my care can make it, I derive a strange feeling out of it, like writing a book in company; a satisfaction of a most singular kind, which has no exact parallel in my life; a something that I suppose to belong to a labourer in art alone, and which has to me a conviction of its being actual truth without its pain that I never could adequately state if I were to try never so hard.[132]

Six months later, Dickens gave Daniel Maclise a similar explanation as to his experience with the role of Wardour.

[131] Dickens to Mary Boyle, February 7, 1857, *Letters,* II, 834.
[132] January 9, 1857, *Letters,* II, 824–825.

I cannot possibly have given you more pleasure through Richard Wardour, than you have given me through your appreciation of it. In that perpetual struggle after an expression of the truth . . . the interest of such a character to me is that it enables me, as it were, *to write a book in company* instead of in my own solitary room, and to feel its effect coming freshly back upon me from the reader. . . . I could blow off my superfluous fierceness in nothing so curious to me.[133]

Like the reviewers, Dickens experienced his performance as fierce, as creative, and somehow as "actual truth."

For Dickens, this experience was probably grounded in Wardour's having the characteristics of a "natural" hero, for whom Dickens had a strong sympathy. These characteristics gave Dickens an opportunity to portray on stage the kind of hero that he had been unwilling to create in his novels lest he offend his readers. Dramatizing inner trials and confusions which he believed inseparable from the making or unmaking of all men, he must have felt that he was giving imaginative life to a fully mature man. He apparently was able to communicate a sense of this inner life to his audience because the "harmony" of the whole production made effective the symbol of the frozen deep and the stock responses associated with it. His appeal to the imagination of the audience, which conveyed the sense of Wardour's complex and powerful inner life, suggests the support of some strong irrational force. The Prologue calls on the stock responses to the Arctic expeditions. Oxenford's review strongly suggests that the call was answered.

The fears and hopes associated with the Franklin expedition were peculiarly high in 1857, because of Lady Franklin's appeals. The question of whether Franklin had succumbed to, or had been victorious over, the stress imposed by the "far-spread-

[133] July 8, 1857, *Letters*, II, 859.

ing frozen waste" could be settled only by an act of faith in "the nature of the men." The government did not erect a statue to Franklin's memory until after a search expedition in 1859 discovered a journal which cleared him of charges of cannibalism; he had died before the expedition had had to abandon its ships. Only then was he credited with having discovered the Northwest Passage and publicly honored. On the occasion of the unveiling of his statue near Waterloo Palace, *The Spectator* reported, "In the Arctic Seas Sir John Franklin's name is that of the first martyr, at Trafalgar—Nelson's. Franklin will always be remembered for his victory over the elements, and not over men." [134] Franklin achieved his "victory" by remaining faithful to an ideal of conduct. Though important in 1857, this victory was uncertain. Even Dickens, despite his strong appeal in 1854 for faith in Franklin's endurance, had admitted that he could not "audaciously set limits to any extremity of desperate distress." The possibility that severe stress could force a strong, heroic man like Franklin to cannibalism raised disturbing questions about the traditional faith in British heroism.

The Arctic expedition in "The Frozen Deep" was associated with the Franklin expedition, though not identified with it. Cannibalism as a temptation would have been suited neither to Tavistock House at Christmas time nor to a character whose role Dickens was to play. The Prologue, however, mentioned Franklin, who had perished while searching for the Northwest Passage, and it directed attention to Wardour, who died after discovering "the passage" at the "northern pole" of his "ice-bound soul." It seems likely that the audience's sense of Wardour's inner life, especially when this inspired strong apprehension, arose from an association between the "Frozen Deep" in Wardour and the Arctic region in which Franklin had perished,

[134] November 17, 1866, p. 1271.

perhaps driven by its stresses to the "last resource." Such an association would explain the strange impact that Dickens made on members of the Royal Party and on "hardened Carpenters." All could have valued the "victory of the better and nobler feelings" because it imaginatively affirmed the faith in the power of the British hero to endure.

Perhaps even more important to Dickens was the affirmation of the faith in the essential goodness of the human heart in a fully mature man, whose maturity had been reached because he had gone through serious inner conflicts. As Dickens described the explorers in his Franklin articles, they were like the heroes in his novels—"too good." Dickens had not mentioned the "suspension of the tender feelings" or the attempted desertion. There is a marked difference between the characterization of the explorers in these articles and Wardour's characterization. The explorers are presented as being threatened solely by a hostile environment, not by any weakness or disorder within themselves. Dickens was fully aware that external forces could destroy a man, either by preventing his development or by unmaking him. In *Hard Times,* forces like those exerted by M'Chokumchild's school prevent Tom Gradgrind and Bitzer from becoming men and almost "unmake" Mr. Gradgrind. In *Little Dorrit,* the Marshalsea, the Circumlocution Office, and Mrs. Clennam's Pharisaism, all exert a comparable force on William Dorrit, Daniel Doyce, and Arthur Clennam. Aldersley, as conceived by Collins, was more like Clennam than Wardour was. Aldersley was a good man, untroubled by inner conflicts and threatened by the hostile Arctic environment and the villainous Wardour. Dickens deliberately destroyed this development so that the "suspended interest" was commanded entirely by Wardour's inner conflicts.

The frozen wastes present Wardour with an opportunity to murder Aldersley, but they are not dramatized as a causal factor in his desire to murder him. This desire, like his indifference to his comrades and his attack on his only friend, arises directly from the "ice-bound" condition of his own soul, from a disordered state of strong passions which have temporarily overpowered or "frozen" the noble sentiments. Wardour would have attempted to murder Aldersley in any environment. The major advantage of the Arctic setting was that it permitted the association between Wardour and popular heroes which gave Dickens' performance the support of stock responses. Both cannibalism and murder arise from what Queen Victoria called the "evil passions" and both indicate the presence of inner confusions, perplexities, and trials. The strong temptation to murder in a good man dramatizes the activity of these passions present in every man. The victory given Wardour by his change of heart affirms the essential goodness of man more strongly than any victory over external forces could have affirmed it. Dressed in rags and near madness, Wardour finally is not "respectable," but he is heroic.

From a modern perspective, there is nothing particularly disreputable about Wardour's inner conflicts; even the mid-Victorians found him "true" and attractive. In 1856, however, Dickens was not certain how an audience would respond to a character like Wardour. He had believed that the hero of an English novel could not be both popular and even faintly disreputable. The canons of respectability, affected by the "smooth gentleman," seemed to place a taboo on the "evil passions" which prompted the conflicts. Performing as Wardour, Dickens not only blew off his own "superfluous fierceness," but also discovered that all sorts of potential readers were not bound by the taboo as he had feared. On the contrary, they approved Wardour as extraordinarily "true" and identified him with the "breadth and depth" of human nature.

Ideas for a new story came into Dickens' head as he lay on the stage, "very excited by the crying of two thousand people over the grave of Richard Wardour." [135] When Dickens wrote the story, *A Tale of Two Cities,* he gave it a hero who was not thoroughly respectable, who was caught in confusions and perplexities that threatened to unmake him. Sydney Carton, like Wardour, finds the power to resolve his inner conflicts in the noble sentiments stirred by the love of a good woman and sacrifices his life to save Charles Darnay, who in many ways is his inferior as a man. The reception of Wardour's stage life and death seems to have exorcised a spectre and permitted the creation first of Carton and later of Pip and Eugene Wrayburn. [136]

[135] Dickens to Miss Coutts, September 5, 1857, *Letters,* II, 876.

[136] For a brief comment on Wardour as the inspiration for Carton see George H. Ford, "Dickens's Notebook and 'Edwin Drood,'" *Nineteenth-Century Fiction,* VI (1952), 275.

Note on the Text of the Play

Establishing a text for the script used in 1857 presents two basic problems. First, the alterations that Collins made in 1866 have to be identified so they can be excluded. Second, some principle has to be adopted for handling the inconsistencies in capitalization, punctuation, and spelling, caused in part by the fair copy having been made by three persons, in part by carelessness.

The alterations that Collins made in 1866 can be identified with a reasonable degree of certainty. Collins removed Nurse Esther, attributed second sight to Clara Burnham, and adjusted the stage directions and dialogue to implement this change. All such alterations were made in black ink and with a broad nib. Most of the fair copy was made in a light ink and with narrow nibs; none of it was made in black ink. To recover a script for the 1857 play, one has to assume that alterations, even a few not directly affecting Nurse Esther or Clara Burnham, in Collins' handwriting, in black ink, and with the broad nib were all made in 1866. This assumption allows such alterations as the transfer in Act III of part of Crayford's dialogue to Steventon to be excluded as an 1866 revision.

Except where inconsistencies in capitalization, punctuation, and spelling seem to offer some clue to the way a word or line was spoken, they have been regularized. For example, Nurse

Esther's dialogue contains "coming" and "cooming," "Southern" and "Southeron." The first inconsistency has been preserved because Dickens made her dialect more heavy in some speeches than in others. The second has been eliminated because where Collins used "Southron" in his original draft, Dickens changed the spelling to "Southern." Dickens did not close the quotation in Mrs. Steventon's opening dialogue; the quotation marks, a dash, and a period have been added: —." The question mark has been added to Rose's speech which follows, "Shall I give you some more tea." Parenthetical comments, forms of direct address, and the like, have been set off with commas. The notes for the prompter and the stage directions are very irregular in the manuscript, beginning sometimes with a capital letter, sometimes with a small letter, with no apparent reason for the difference. These have been regularized. In the dialogue, the irregular capitalization of some significant words—like "snow," "ice," and "expedition"—probably indicates the emphasis intended for the spoken part. Because Dickens sometimes used capitalization for emphasis, such inconsistencies have been left unchanged.

The Frozen Deep

THE FROZEN DEEP

In Three Acts

The Scene of the First Act, an old Country House in Devonshire (Telbin)

The Scene of the Second Act, a Hut in the Arctic Regions (Stanfield)

The Scene of the Third Act, a Cavern on the coast of Newfoundland (Stanfield)

Period, The Present Time

Time occupied in representation—Two hours and a half.

The Prompt-Book

Dram: Pers:

Captain Ebsworth, of the Sea Mew	F. Pigott [1]
Captain Helding, of the Wanderer	Alfred Dickens
Lieutenant Crayford	Mark Lemon
Frank Aldersley	Wilkie Collins
Richard Wardour	Charles Dickens
Lieutenant Steventon	Charley [Dickens, Jr.]
John Want	Augustus Egg
Bateson ⎫ Two of the Sea Mew's people ⎧ Edward Hogarth	
Darker ⎭ ⎩ Frederick Evans	

Officers and Sailors

Mrs. Steventon	Ellen Hogarth
Rose Ebsworth	Katie [Dickens]
Lucy Crayford	Georgina [Hogarth]
Clara Burnham	Mary [Dickens]
Nurse Esther	Mrs. Wills

Maid

[1] Edward Pigott played the role of Captain Ebsworth, but Dickens listed him in the MS as F. Pigott.

95

Prologue

(*Curtain rises. Mists and darkness. Soft music throughout.*)
One savage footprint on the lonely shore,
Where one man listen'd to the surge's roar;
Not all the winds that stir the mighty sea
Can ever ruffle in the memory.
If such its interest and thrall, O then
Pause on the footprints of heroic men,
Making a garden of the desert wide
Where PARRY conquer'd and FRANKLIN died.

To that white region where the Lost lie low,
Wrapp'd in their mantles of eternal snow;
Unvisited by change, nothing to mock
Those statues sculptured in the icy rock,
We pray your company; that hearts as true
(Though nothings of the air) may live for you;
Nor only yet that on our little glass
A faint reflection of those wilds may pass,
But, that the secrets of the vast Profound
Within us, an exploring hand may sound,
Testing the region of the ice-bound soul,
Seeking the passage at its northern pole,
Soft'ning the horrors of its wintry sleep,
Melting the surface of that 'Frozen Deep.'

Vanish, ye mists! But ere this gloom departs,
And to the union of three sister arts
We give a winter evening, good to know
That in the charms of such another show,
That in the fiction of a friendly play,
The Arctic sailors, too, put gloom away,
Forgot their long night, saw no starry dome,
Hail'd the warm sun, and were again at Home.

Vanish ye mists! Not yet do we repair
To the still country of the piercing air;
But seek, before we cross the troubled Seas,
An English hearth and Devon's waving trees.[2]

[2] The Prologue, written by Dickens, was spoken by John Forster during the Tavistock House performances and by Dickens during the Gallery of Illustration and Manchester performances. It is not included in the M.A. 81 collection. The version printed here is taken from *The Letters of Charles Dickens*, ed. Georgina Hogarth and Mamie Dickens (New York, n.d.), pp. 522–523.

THE FROZEN DEEP

Act the First

Act I*

(*Scene* 1. *A pleasant room in a country-house with an old fashioned bay window in the flat, looking out over autumn corn fields on a village church embosomed in woods. This prospect is supposed to be seen shortly before sunset. The room very comfortably and prettily furnished. Flowers about. A few flower pots on a Stand. A tea-table with tea things on it. Two little Work Tables with baskets of work on them, etc., etc. A bird in a cage. Mrs. Steventon and Rose discovered. Maid enters with newspaper from the post. Is going to give it to Rose. Mrs. Steventon beckons for it and it is given to her.*)

ROSE: Any news, Caroline?

MRS. STEVENTON: (*Reading*) "Arrived, the Fortune from Valparaiso. The Ariel from Jamaica. (*Spoken*) The Sisters from Liverpool for California, eight days out. Reported drifting among ice at Sea, waterlogged and abandoned, the Hope—." (*Hurriedly and repressing a shudder*) No, Rose—no news to interest *us*.

ROSE: Shall I give you some more tea? (*Mrs. S. declines.*) Where are Clara and Lucy?

* (*Before ringing up, see the Furniture Properties correct by the list. See the colored lights ready at the back. See the working sky ready. See that Lucy Crayford has a book. See that Clara Burnham has dried flowers in an envelope. See that Maid has folded Newspaper ready. See that basket, scissors and watering pot are ready. A. P. S.*)

Mrs. Steventon: Upstairs. I think Clara is asleep. (*Enter Maid with watering-pot, scissors, and basket. Mrs. S. and she water and arrange flowers as the Dialogue proceeds.*) Rose, I have been doubting lately whether it was wise for us four to shut ourselves up in this lonely old house while our natural protectors are away from us in the expedition to the Arctic Seas.

Rose: What could we do better than wait here together till they come back? Have we any friends to go to whom we should honestly like to live with? Would it have been pleasant for you to go home after your husband had sailed with the expedition?

Mrs. Steventon: Home! Where they have turned their backs on me for marrying a poor man! I go home and hear my husband despised?

Rose: And I with no mother alive; with my father like your husband, away with the Arctic ships—where could I have been happier than here with my dearest and oldest friend, Lucy Crayford?

Mrs. Steventon: And Lucy certainly had no home to go to. Her only near relation in the world is her brother, who is serving in the expedition.

Rose: Well; you see there are three of us at any rate who could have done no better than come here and make one household of it. As for the fourth, as for Clara—

Mrs. Steventon: Clara's situation is different in one respect. It is not her father, or her brother, or her husband, who is away, but her husband that is to be. Then again, Clara has a mother alive—

Rose: A mother who has gone abroad, and married again—a mother, who has never forgiven Clara for objecting to a foreign Stepfather! (*Exit Maid with watering-pot, etc.*)

Mrs. Steventon: I dare say you may be right, my dear, (*comes down, takes her work from her work table, and returns with it to tea-table*) but I cannot help doubting still whether all we women do not make each other unduly anxious by being constantly together here, and living in perfect solitude. As long as we had News from the Expedition it was very well to have no society but our own—but now, when more than a year has passed, and no tidings from those fatal regions have reached us, I think we ought to see other sights from day to day, besides the sight of our own sad faces.

ROSE: (*Covering the bird*) I can't say that seeing company would be any relief to *my* mind. I have no heart for paying visits and making new acquaintances, while my father is risking his life, commanding the Expedition in the Polar Seas. (*Re-enter Maid and exit with the bird.*) I shrink from going into the world and seeing girls of my own age, with Parents living always near them, in the safety and quietness of Home. I should envy their lot, I should repine at my own—I who have not had my father's arms round me for three long years! I am fond of gaieties, Caroline; I like being nicely dressed, I like being admired, I like Music and Dancing; but I must have my father near me, or I can never enjoy myself as I ought. Once let me get him back, and O what dresses I'll have, what dances I'll go to, what a charming life of gaiety mine shall be from morning to night!

MRS. STEVENTON: Yours is an enviable disposition, Rose. If I had your courage and your hopefulness—

ROSE: Determine, as I do, and as Lucy does, not to despair. Shall I ring and have these things taken away? (*Rises and rings the bell; then takes her work at her table.*) I wish I could communicate a little of the hopefulness that you envy so, to Clara.

MRS. STEVENTON: I believe nobody has any real influence over Clara, except that strange old Scotch Nurse of hers, whom she is so unaccountably fond of.

Rose: Yes, Lucy has influence over her; but I must say, I wish her faithful Highland Nurse—

Mrs. Steventon: Not Highland, Rose.

(*Scotch Music, "Wandering Willie" once.*)

Rose: Highland by descent and birth, I think, though Lowland by usage and education—it doesn't matter—Scotch in any case. I was going to say, I wish her faithful Scotch Nurse was safely back among her own people. Clara is naturally excitable and nervous; and that unfortunate old woman with her perpetual prophesying and her barbarous nonsense about the Second Sight, does her young mistress all the harm in the world. Lucy thinks so, and Lucy is always right.

Mrs. Steventon: I am afraid Nurse is likely to do the Servants harm too. Only last week, she frightened them all by seeming to be in a kind of fit at dinner. I was sent for, and she stared at me as if I had been a stranger, and shuddered all over, and said the Power of the Sight was on her—meaning, I suppose, the Second Sight that one reads about, in books on the Highlands.

Rose: I hope she is not in another fit now. Nobody seems inclined to answer the bell. (*Scotch Music, "Wandering Willie." Enter Nurse Esther.*)

Nurse Esther: Wha' rings?

Mrs. Steventon: No, no, Nurse, we don't want you. Send the Maid to take away the tray.

Nurse Esther: No' want me? The day may come, Mistress, when ye'll just be doon on your knees, begging me to speak! Where's your husband? (*To Rose*) Where's your father? Where's Lucy Crayford's brother? Where's my nurse-child Clara's plighted lover? Lost a' lost, i' the lands o' Ice and Snow! Wha' sees them and follows them in the spirit? Wha' can give ye news of them when a' earthly tidings fail? Southern leddy, when ye want next to hear o' yer husband, ye'll want me.

ROSE: (*Coaxingly*) Yes, yes, Nurse Esther; but you know, being Southern ladies, we don't believe in the Second Sight.

NURSE ESTHER: Don't believe in the Second Sight? Look at me! No believe my deary, when I stand here afore you wi' the power o' th' Sight coming strong on me the noo'—coming aye stronger and aye stronger sin' the purple morn, but no' at its height yet! Can you look me in the face with they bright black een o' yours and no feel a shuddering at the roots o' your hair, no feel a creeping ower your dainty flesh? No, no, no; ye know me too weel, Missy. (*Quickly changing two knives which Mrs. S. has put across*) Air ye for bluid that ye put twa' blades crosswise! (*Becoming dreamy*) It's aye cooming on me, it's aye cooming! I ha' warned ye I shall speak o' the lost men who are wandering ower the Icy North.

MRS. STEVENTON: (*To Rose*) Can't you persuade her to be quiet? (*Coming to work-table.*)

ROSE: I don't like to risk offending her.

NURSE ESTHER: I warn ye baith that afore the neecht's ower I shall speak. When the Moon is rising, and the warning chimes are ringing out fra' yon auld Kirk, bide in this room and hear me. Mark my words, dearies! When the chimes are ringing. Mark my words. (*Exit.*)

(*Scotch Music repeated—"Wandering Willie." Maid enters, clears the tea-things, puts away tea-table and two chairs. Then exit Maid, and Music dies away. Mrs. S. and Rose wind off a skein of silk, during the remainder of their dialogue at Rose's work-table.*)

MRS. STEVENTON: I wonder Clara in all these years since her childhood has not civilized Nurse Esther a little—Ah, dear Lucy! Like a rainbow after the clouds!

(*Enter Lucy.*)

Rose: (*To her*) Darling, have you seen Clara since dinner time?

Lucy: I sat and read to her 'till she fell asleep. Let me say to you two, my dears, that I am getting so uneasy about her, that I sometimes think of sending to London for the best Doctor.

Rose: But the Doctor here—

Lucy: My dear, the Doctor here is a very estimable, industrious man; but he does not understand diseases of the mind. From month to month, I have seen, as I now see, Clara still wasting, still growing paler and paler, still dreaming by night and talking by day, in a manner that shocks and alarms me.

Mrs. Steventon: You ought to remember that she was always nervous and fanciful from a child. And you ought to make allowances for the influence of that superstitious old Nurse over her.

Lucy: (*Thoughtfully*) Yes.

Rose: Recollect too, the loss of all news of the Expedition in which she has as dear an interest as any of us.

Lucy: Dearer.

Mrs. Steventon: (*Warmly*) Dearer than mine? Can a girl like Clara be fonder of her Lover than I am of my Husband?

Lucy: We will not discuss the question. (*Sits at Mrs. S.'s work-table.*) I make full allowance for Clara's excessive sensitiveness, for the bad influence of her Nurse, and for the effect on her of the suspense under which we are all suffering; but still I cannot account to myself for the state of nervous depression and irritation into which she has fallen. I suspected she had some secret sorrow or anxiety when she first came here; and I feel sure that I was right.

Mrs. Steventon: Perhaps she has said something to you?

Lucy: Not a word.

Rose: And yet you are her favorite. She will do things for

you, that she will do for neither of us. If she really ever had a secret sorrow, she would have confided it to you, long ago.

LUCY: All dispositions, my dear, are not so open as yours. But we had better change the subject.

MRS. STEVENTON: Why?

LUCY: Because Clara is coming down stairs. (*Goes near the door*) I hear her footstep.

(*Enter Clara Burnham, hurried and agitated.*)

CLARA: Where are you all? (*Sits.*) Why did you leave me, Lucy? I hate and dread being alone—and you all forsake me. You care for nobody—you forget everything.

MRS. STEVENTON: We thought you were asleep in your own room.

CLARA: Was I to sleep there for ever?

ROSE: If you had only rung when you woke—

CLARA: Nurse Esther would have answered the bell, I suppose. And what then?

LUCY: (*Aside to Mrs. S. and Rose*) She has awakened in one of her nervous fits. If you will leave her to me, I think I can soothe her.*

MRS. STEVENTON: You were right, about sending to London for some one. Let us go into the Music Room, Rose. She always gets better when she is like this, if she hears music. Clara dear, don't send for Nurse Esther any more tonight. Send for me. (*Exeunt Mrs. S. and Rose.*)

(*Lucy, after looking at Clara for a moment, takes a chair and seats herself by Clara's side.*)

CLARA: Don't mind me. I'm used to being left alone. Nurse will come to me, I dare say. Go to the piano with the other two.

LUCY: Hush! Hush! Don't talk any more 'till you feel easier

* (*Setting sun ready to work. Gas ready to turn down. Red lights ready. Piano Music ready.*)

and quieter.* (*Setting sun appears in view, and the notes of the piano are heard softly from the adjoining room.*) O look at this, my love, look at this with me! O dear Heaven, how tenderly the last red glow lingers on the corn fields, and how softly the shadows are stealing over the distant woods! What a gentleness in that farewell glory of the day that is leaving us! What a harmony of Earthly sounds answers that great silent harmony of colors in the Palace of the western clouds! Think how many aching hearts the sight of that mighty calmness, that Divine glory, shall soothe to repose this night! Think and look! Look reverently and thankfully, while that great tranquillity which breathes so mercifully over the Earth, breathes also over you!

CLARA: I must be happier before I can feel it, Lucy. Your eyes look only at the brightness and the beauty. Mine see the fading daylight, and the gathering gloom.

LUCY: The Daylight renews itself, and the gloom vanishes with the morning. (*Takes chair.*) I wish, my love, I knew how to make you look and speak a little more cheerfully!

CLARA: We have no cause for cheerfulness.

LUCY: We have no cause for despair.

CLARA: Do you still say, Not yet?

LUCY: I still say, Not yet. The same uncertainty which hangs over the fate of your promised husband, hangs also over the fate of my only brother. And still I say, Not even yet.

CLARA: Three years have passed, Lucy, since they left us. If a fourth goes by, and we hear nothing of them, will you still speak as you have spoken now? [3]

* (*Lower gas. Setting Sun worked. Red light. Music, Piano in next room. Heard at intervals until "my sorrow looks so base and mean."*)

[3] This and Lucy's speech which follows were added on the back of a leaf, revised by Dickens, and then deleted. The deletion appears to have been made by Collins when he was making the 1866 alterations, but cannot be dated with certainty.

LUCY: No, my love. I shall perhaps surprise you by giving bolder advice. If another year passes without tidings of the Expedition, new ships will be fitted out, and a rescuing party will be sent to search for the lost men. Should the day for that sad necessity arrive, then, Clara, I shall be the first to own that we have waited here in solitude and resignation long enough. I shall then say to you and to Caroline and to Rose;—the time for patience is past. Let us follow the rescuing party along the shores of America as far as women may go, and let us be the first to meet the ships of the Seekers when they come out from the Arctic Seas. In the meantime, I repeat, let us still be patient, let us still hope! (*Clara to go back.*)

CLARA: (*Abruptly*) Lucy, have you ever known a great sorrow?

LUCY: Examine your own heart, my dear, and you will hardly need to ask me that question.

CLARA: How?

LUCY: You have not known me longer than you have known Caroline and Rose, and yet you say, and I believe you, that you love me like a sister, while you only love them like friends. I am no kinder to you than they are. Why should you have preferred me from the first?

CLARA: Because—

LUCY: Let me answer for you. Because you felt that some great sorrow had set its mark on me. You were drawn towards me by true instinct, and the secret of that instinct is, that you yourself—

CLARA: No! no!

LUCY: That you yourself have a great sorrow. (*Clara hides her face.*) A sorrow which you have confessed to no one—a sorrow that guided you to me, as to another woman who had suffered also. There has been sympathy between us because there has been secret trouble on either side. I do not ask you for your confidence, my dear. I only ask, if this is the truth? (*Music stops.*)

CLARA: Oh, Lucy, you know it is the truth.

LUCY: (*Music re-commences.*) Perhaps my own experience might one day help me in guiding you. I can tell you what it has been in very few words. You have once or twice wondered why I was still a single woman. My dear, I shall always remain what I am now, because the man I loved with all my heart and soul, the man to whom I was once engaged to be married is—

CLARA: Dead?

LUCY: To *me*. Married. Don't be angry with *him*, Clara,—he was not to blame. He had not met her when he engaged himself to me. I don't think he knew his own mind then. I don't think he ever suspected how dearly I loved him. 'Twas I that broke it all off—he was honourable and would have redeemed his promise—'twas my fault—perhaps I was hasty and jealous—but all that is over now. My thoughts and ways of life have altered since then. I think I have learnt to be more patient and more regardful of others than I was. You must not suppose mine to be a romantic story that is to have a fine, romantic end. This (*touching her heart*) is the commonplace end, my dear.

CLARA: O! Lucy. My poor selfish sorrow looks so base and mean beside your better one. (*Music stops.*)

LUCY: Base and mean, my pet? (*Puts Clara back from her, and looks her steadily in the face.*) I see no baseness or meanness here! Clara! Have you not given all your heart to Frank Aldersley? Do you not love him as every woman loves her promised husband?

CLARA: Love him! (*Takes a letter from her bosom.*) Look where I keep his last letter to me. (*Opens the envelope.*) Look in there!

LUCY: Withered flowers!

CLARA: * All that is left of the nosegay he gave me, the last time we met. Love him! (*Takes Lucy's hand and places it on her heart.*) Let it answer for itself!

LUCY: Then why talk of baseness and meanness?

CLARA: Let me rest my head on your shoulder. I can speak to you better so.

LUCY: Ah! rest your head, my love. Think my shoulder is only the back of a chair. (*The melody from the adjoining room, which has hitherto been heard indistinctly below the voices of the speakers, stops for a moment, then changes to "Those Evening Bells." A pause in the dialogue until the Second Verse has been sung.*) † Clara, are you crying? Don't speak now, if it distresses you. (*Music stops.*)

CLARA: No. I am going to tell you. I am going to tell you about the time when my father was alive, and I was a little girl. We lived in a pretty country house in Kent, near a great park. Our nearest neighbor was a gentleman named Wardour, who owned the park. He was one of my father's old friends, and his only son, Richard,‡ was some years older than I.[4]

LUCY: He was still your playmate, I suppose? And you liked him?

* (*Symphony of.*) This has been written over a deleted prompt note: (*Music "Oft in the stilly night," ready*). It seems to refer to the "Symphony of 'Those Evening Bells'" that was to be used in a few seconds.

† (*Sun sinks. Gas lower. Red lights gradually withdrawn. Piano Music, "River, River" ready.*)

‡ (*Turn gas still lower. Piano Music, "River, River."*)

[4] This last phrase and the next three speeches were heavily deleted and revised by Collins to remove the suggestions of childhood fondness and to suggest an ambiguous, adult passion. Again, these appear to have been part of his 1866 alterations, but they cannot be dated with certainty. The original prompt-book reading is given here.

CLARA: As a playmate, yes. He was—oh so terribly head-strong and passionate!—but a generous, affectionate boy in spite of his faults of temper. *I* ought to know that better than any one —he was so fond of me.

LUCY: Fond of you when you were a child?

CLARA: Fond of me when I was more than a child. He never spoke of the fondness, but I could not help seeing it. I did all I could to show that I was willing to be like a sister to him, and that I could be nothing else. (*Music stops.*) He did not understand me, or he would not—I can't say which. There was a strange, rough bashfulness about him. What could I do? He never spoke out—he seemed to treat me as if our future lives had been provided for while we were children. My situation was a very trying one, was it not, Lucy?

LUCY: *Did you never ask your father to end the difficulty for you?

CLARA: He was suffering, at that time, under the illness which afterwards caused his death, and was very unfit to agitate himself by breaking off the intercourse between his daughter and his old friend's only son. Knowing this, I hesitated—unfortunately until it was too late.

LUCY: How too late?

CLARA: Richard, I should have told you, was, like Frank, in the navy. One Spring day he came to our house to take leave of us before he joined his ship. I thought he was gone, and went into the conservatory—when he suddenly returned and said in his rough quick way—"Clara, I am going to the African coast. If I live, I shall come back promoted, and we both know what will happen then!" He kissed me. I was half frightened, half angry—

* (*Piano Music heard softly, at intervals, until "It was Richard War-dour."*)

and, before I could compose myself to say a word, he was gone. I ought to have spoken—I ought not to have let him go as I did. It was not honourable, not kind towards him. I reproached myself bitterly at the time for my want of courage and frankness —I reproach myself still—I always shall reproach myself to my dying day!

Lucy: Could you not write to him?

Clara: I did write—but his after conduct showed that he never received the letter. He was away more than two years. In that time, Frank Aldersley and I met—and—and—you know what happened,—you know that we were engaged. I was so happy! Months and months passed, and not a thought of Richard Wardour ever entered my head, till, one winter morning, I heard that he had come back. (*Music "River, River" again.*) And, Lucy, two days afterwards, his own lips told me that he had come back to make me his wife! Think of my terror and confusion, and remorse. I shrank away from him, and stammered out a few words—very few, but they were enough to tell him what had happened. Lucy! (*Music "River, River" again.*) I tremble when I think of his face. It comes across me in my dreams and makes me as frightened in the darkness as a child.* How dark it is now!

Lucy: Not darker than usual, my child.

Clara: His awful, awful look of fury and despair—his deep heavy breaths that came from him in the silence, as he crushed down the passion within him—the parting words he spoke, the last I ever heard from his lips. (*Music stops.*) "The time may come when I shall forgive *you*," he said,† "but the man who has robbed me of you shall rue the day when you and he first met."

* (*The stage gets darker. Turn gas lower still.*)
† (*Moonrise and moonlight ready.*)

(*Music re-commences.*) He stood looking at me for a minute— then turned away suddenly and went out. From that time to this I have never seen him again.

LUCY: And never heard of him?

CLARA: The worst, the worst is to come. I heard of him but once, and that was on the night of my parting with Frank. I was asking Frank about the two ships of the Expedition and who was to sail in them. He told me about the officers of his own ship, the "Sea Mew"—and then he spoke of having visited the other ship, the "Wanderer," and of making acquaintance with some of the officers on board. He said they were all pleasant men, with the exception of one moody silent stranger, who had only that day joined as a volunteer. "Did you find out who he was?", I asked carelessly. "I only found out his name," said Frank. "It was Richard Wardour"! *

LUCY: My love! How you are trembling! Shall I ring for lights?

CLARA: No, no—only put your arm round me—let me feel you near me. Oh, Lucy! They have sailed away together—away to the eternal ice and snow—the man who is to marry me and the man whose heart I have broken!

LUCY: In separate ships—you said yourself they were in separate ships.

CLARA: But in the same Expedition—to share the same perils —to be united in one ship, if an accident happens to the other— to be at deadly enmity together if my name is ever mentioned between them.

LUCY: No, no—let us hope, let us pray, not. Did you mention Frank's name at your last interview with Richard Wardour?

* (*The stage gets quite dark. The music in the next room stops. Moon begins to rise. Moonlight gradually shewn. Music "Those Evening Bells" ready.*)

CLARA: He gave me no time to mention it, even if I had had the courage to do so.

LUCY: Was your engagement with Frank generally known?

CLARA: It was kept a secret because we were uncertain when he would rise sufficiently high in his profession to marry. Except my mother and my uncle, no one knew of our engagement at the time when the Expedition sailed.

(*Enter Esther at the back of the sofa. Music "Wandering Willie" changing at "D'ye hear! D'ye hear!" into "Those Evening Bells."*)

LUCY: Thank God for that! When Frank told you about his joining the ship, did you say anything?

CLARA: I had not the courage to say a word. But Lucy! one chance syllable between them might discover everything! Oh, for any tidings, any tidings!

NURSE ESTHER: (*From the back of the stage*) Tidings! I' this hoose, ye'll get na' tidings mair.

LUCY: Who's that!

NURSE ESTHER: The men are lost, a' lost; i' the land o' ice and snow. On the land o' ice and snow they shall never be found again!

CLARA: Nurse, *nurse!* What have you seen? How do you know it? Let me go, Lucy—I want to ask *her* something.*

LUCY: No! Stop with me. Nurse! If you have any regard for your child, be silent. You agitate, you destroy her by talking in that way. Lights. Lights!—pull down the blind. Keep out that cold spectral moonlight.

NURSE ESTHER: (*Gets on the sofa, as if to pull down the blind.*) If I do your bidding, it's for her sake, not for yours. Southern leddy, the Second Sight is a truth. The power of it was on me the morn, and is on me the noo'. Said I not I would speak

* (*Chimes ready.*)

wi' the gloaming, when the moon was rising, and the bells were ringing from yon auld Kirk? D'ye hear! D'ye hear!

(*The moonlight falls on her face. The Chimes ring in the distance the air of "Those Evening Bells." The piano in the next room takes up the tune, and the voices of Rose and Mrs. Steventon are heard softly, singing the words of the melody. This effect of music lasts till the fall of the curtain.*)

CLARA: Nurse Esther! Speak to me, nurse! Does the Sight show you Frank?

LUCY: Clara! Clara!

NURSE ESTHER: Doos the Sight show me Frank? Aye! and anither beside Frank. I see the lamb i' the grasp o' the lion. I see your bonnie bird alone wi' the hawk. I see you and all around you crying bluid! The stain is on you! Oh my bairn, my bairn, the stain o' that bluid is on *you!*

(*Clara drops on Lucy's bosom with a faint cry. The Curtain falls.*)

END OF THE FIRST ACT

THE FROZEN DEEP

Act the Second

Act II*

(*Scene: A Hut in the Arctic Regions. Door in flat, opening on the bleak polar prospect, where the snow is seen to fall incessantly, as often as the door is opened. Through an aperture in the roof, the snow falls drearily, at intervals, on the floor, throughout the act. On one side of the hut, 2 sleeping berths and a rude fire. On the other side, a doorway, with a piece of an old sail hanging across it, communicating with an inner hut. Hanging from the roof, a hammock. Icicles have formed in the interstices of the walls. On the stage, an old cask to serve for a table, with a pestle and mortar on it. Also a chest or two. Bateson discovered dozing at the fire. As Act Drop rises, Music "Berger." Enter Lieutenant Crayford from the inner hut.*)

CRAYFORD: Jump up, Bateson! It's your turn to be relieved. Darker! (*A sailor enters from the inner hut.*) It's your watch. Look lively, my man, look lively. Anything to report, Bateson? (*Walks about.*)

BATESON: †Nothing, your honour, except that it's pinching cold. (*Exit into inner hut.*)

* (*Before ringing up, see Properties correct, according to list. See the People of the Sea Mew ready in the 1st Entrance. O. P. See Snow ready —at the back, and at the Roof, 2 places. See that Crayford has a paper message for Steventon, a paper and instructions for Captain Helding, and a paper of lots. See that John Want has a watch. See sledge, knapsacks, and wrappers of travelling party ready at back.*)

† (*Snow ready.*)

CRAYFORD: And that's no news in the Arctic Regions, with the thermometer below zero indoors. My poor dear sister, Lucy, what would she say, with her horror of cold, if she knew what our temperature was here! (*Snow behind window.*) Look out, Darker, and report what weather we have this morning.

(*Darker opens the door. The snow is seen falling heavily.*)

DARKER: The usual weather, Sir. (*Shuts the door, sighs, and exit.*)

CRAYFORD: (*Sighing too*) Ah! the usual weather! No change in these dreary regions! Well, well—duty, duty! Let me see, what have I to do? (*Looks round and sees the pestle and mortar.*) Oh, here are these wretched bones to be pounded for soup. I must rouse the cook. (*Calling*) John Want! That fellow little thinks how useful he is in keeping up my spirits. No matter how the cold pinches, he always amuses me. John Want!—the most inveterate croaker and grumbler in the world; and yet, according to his own account, the only cheerful man in the whole ship's company. John Want! John Want!

JOHN WANT: (*Speaking from the hammock*) Give me some more sleep!

CRAYFORD: Not a wink, you mutinous rascal! Rouse up!

JOHN WANT: (*Peeping out*) Lord, Lord! here's all my breath on my blanket. Icicles if you please, Sir, all round my mouth and all over my blanket. Every time I've snored I've frozen something. (*Gets out and goes to the fire.*) When a man gets the cold into him to that extent that he ices his own bed, it can't last much longer. *I* don't grumble.

CRAYFORD: Come here, Sir, and set to work on this mortar. What are you doing there?

JOHN WANT: (*Holding his chin over the fire*) Thawing my beard, Sir.

CRAYFORD: Come here, I say! What the devil are you about now?

JOHN WANT: (*At the fire with a watch in his hand*) Thawing my watch, Sir. It's been under my pillow all night, and the cold has stopped it. Cheerful, wholesome, bracing sort of climate to live in, isn't it, Sir? But *I* don't grumble.

CRAYFORD: No, we all know that. You are the only cheerful man of the ship's company. Look here. Are these bones pounded small enough?

JOHN WANT: (*Taking the pestle and mortar*) You'll excuse me, Sir, but how very hollow your voice sounds this morning!

CRAYFORD: Keep your remarks about my voice to yourself, and answer my question about the bones.

JOHN WANT: Well, Sir, they'll take a trifle more pounding. I'll do my best with them today, Sir, for your sake.

CRAYFORD: What do you mean?

JOHN WANT: I don't think I shall have the honour of making much more bone soup for you, Sir. Do you think yourself you'll last long, Sir? I don't, saving your presence. I think about another week or ten days will do for us all. (*Bateson approaches from the inner hut.*) This man looks bad, too, don't he, Sir? He was half an hour cutting one log of wood yesterday. His legs are swelling—and he loses his temper at trifles. I give *him* another day or two. (*Snow from Roof.*) I give the best of us a week. (*Looks up.*)

CRAYFORD: (*To Bateson*) Now then, my man, what is it?

BATESON: A message from Capt. Ebsworth, Sir.

CRAYFORD: Well?

BATESON: Captain Ebsworth is worse than ever with his freezing pains, Sir, this morning. He wants to see you, and give you some important directions, immediately.

CRAYFORD: I will go at once. Rouse the doctor. We shall want all the help he can give us. (*Exit, followed by Bateson.*)

JOHN WANT: (*Pounding the bones*) Rouse the doctor? Suppose the doctor should be frozen? He hadn't a ha'porth of warmth in him last night, and his voice sounded like a whisper in a speaking trumpet. (*Pours the bones into a saucepan.*) In with you, and flavour the hot water, if you can! When I remember that I was once an apprentice at a pastry cook's; when I think of the gallons of turtle soup that this hand has stirred up in a jolly hot kitchen; and when I find myself now mixing bones and hot water for soup, and turning into ice as fast as I can, if I wasn't of a cheerful disposition, I should feel inclined to grumble. John Want! John Want! Whatever had you done with your natural senses when you made up your mind to go to sea?

ALDERSLEY: (*Speaking from his bed place*) Who's that croaking over the fire?

JOHN WANT: Croaking? You don't find your own voice at all altered for the worse, do you, Mr. Frank? (*Aside*) I don't give *him* more than another six hours. He's one of your grumblers.

ALDERSLEY: What are you doing there?

JOHN WANT: Making bone soup, Sir, and wondering why I ever went to sea.

ALDERSLEY: Oh, it's John Want,—well, and why did you go to sea?

JOHN WANT: I'm not certain, Sir, sometimes I think it was a natural perversity. Sometimes I think it was false pride at getting over sea-sickness. Sometimes I think it was reading Robinson Crusoe, and books warning of me not to go to sea.

ALDERSLEY: (*Composing himself to sleep again*) Everybody gets over sea-sickness.

JOHN WANT: (*Stirring up the soup*) Not as *I* did, Sir. I got over sea-sickness by dint of hard eating. I was a passenger on board a packet boat, Sir, when first I saw blue water. A nasty lopp of a sea come on just at dinner time, and I began to feel queer the moment the soup was put on the table. "Sick?" says the Captain. "Rather, Sir," says I. "Will you try my cure?" says the Captain. "Certainly, Sir," says I. "Is your heart in your mouth yet?" says the Captain. "Not quite, Sir," says I. "Mock turtle soup!" says the Captain—and helps me. I swallow a couple of spoonfuls, and turn as white as a sheet. The Captain cocks his eye at me. "Go on deck, Sir," says he, "get rid of the soup, and then come back to the cabin"—I got rid of the soup, and came back to the cabin. "Cod's head and shoulder," says the Captain—and helps me. "I can't stand it, Sir," says I. "You must," says the Captain, "because it's the cure." I crammed down a mouthful, and turned paler than ever. "Go on deck," says the Captain, "get rid of the cod's head,—come back to the cabin." Off I go, and * back I come. "Boiled leg of mutton and trimmings," says the Captain, and helps me. "No fat, Sir," says I. "Fat's the cure," says the Captain and makes me eat it. "Lean's the cure," says the Captain and makes me eat it. "Steady?" says the Captain. "Sick," says I. "Go on deck," says the Captain. "Get rid of the boiled leg of mutton and trimmings, and come back to the cabin." Off I go, staggering—back I come more dead than alive. "Devilled kidneys," says the Captain. I shut my eyes, and got 'em down. "Cure's beginning," says the Captain. "Mutton chop and pickles." I shut my eyes and got *them* down. "Boiled Ham and Cayenne Pepper," says the Captain. "Glass of Stout and cranberry tart. Want to go on deck again?"—"No, Sir," says I. "Cure's done," says the Captain. "Never you give in to your stomach and your stomach will end in giving in to *you*." (*Music, "Begone Dull Care"—once only. Exit into inner hut with the soup. Enter Crayford.*)

  * (*Music "Begone Dull Care," ready.*)

CRAYFORD: Steventon! *

STEVENTON: (*Rising from his bed place*) Here. Anything wanted?

CRAYFORD: The Captain is too ill to get up. He has been giving me some very important and very unexpected directions. There is to be a change at last in our wretched lives here.

STEVENTON: A change! What change?

CRAYFORD: The crew of the "Sea Mew" here, and the crew of the "Wanderer" on the other side of the hillock yonder (*snow*) are to be united today in this hut. Send a man with that message from our Captain to Captain Helding of the "Wanderer." (*Gives a paper to Steventon, who retires to the back of the hut, rouses a sailor and equips him for going out.*) Frank! Frank Aldersley!

ALDERSLEY: (*Rising from his bed place*) Yes.

CRAYFORD: One of the officer's chests had a backgammon board and dice in it, just before we abandoned the "Sea Mew"?

ALDERSLEY: It was my chest. I have got them still in my berth here. Shall I get them?

CRAYFORD: I only want the dice and the box for casting lots.

(*Frank gets the dice, and Steventon, having dismissed the messenger, returns to the front.*)

STEVENTON: (*Observing the dice-box as Frank gives it to Crayford*) Dice! Are we going to gamble at the North Pole?

CRAYFORD: No, no. (*To Frank*) I am afraid, Frank, you are hardly strong enough, after your illness, to make one of an exploring party.

ALDERSLEY: I am ready to venture. Any risk is better than pining and perishing here. (*Draws a stool to the fire, and sits down before it. Gradually falls asleep. Crayford seats himself at the opposite side of the stage from Frank.*)

* (*Snow ready.*)

STEVENTON: (*Pointing at Frank and seating himself by Crayford*) He doesn't think of danger—he thinks of nothing but getting back to his sweetheart. By the way, who does poor Dennam's duty now in the "Wanderer's" hut?

CRAYFORD: One of the best officers and one of the hardiest men in the Queen's Navy—Richard Wardour.

STEVENTON: *Your liking for that man amazes me, Crayford.

CRAYFORD: Remember that I have had peculiar opportunities of knowing him. I sailed from England with him, in the "Wanderer," and was only transferred to the "Sea Mew" long after we were locked up in the Ice. I was Richard Wardour's companion on board ship for months, and I learnt there to do him justice.

STEVENTON: You can't deny the violence of his temper?

CRAYFORD: I don't deny it.

STEVENTON: Or the sullenness of his disposition?

CRAYFORD: Yes, I deny that. He is not naturally a sullen man. Under all his outward defects there beats a great and generous heart. You are prejudiced against Richard Wardour from not knowing enough of him.

STEVENTON: Then Frank there, is prejudiced too—for he agrees with me.†

CRAYFORD: ‡And what opportunities has Frank had of judging? I have never seen him in Wardour's society for five minutes together. (*Lowering his voice.*)

STEVENTON: (*Looking at Frank*) You needn't lower your voice. He's asleep and dreaming, I dare say.

CRAYFORD: He dreams a great deal, does he not?

* (*Music "When thou sittest gazing," ready. Vision ready. See Clara Burnham at the fire.*)

† (*Music, "When thou sittest gazing on the red fire blazing," until "and making others hope, God bless her!"—then changing into "River, River," until Crayford speaks to Captain Helding.*)

‡ (*Snow ready.*)

† (*Snow ready.*)

STEVENTON: Yes, and always of the poor girl he is engaged to be married to. I dare say he is dreaming of her now. (*The figure of Clara Burnham appears in the fire, watching Frank as he sleeps.*) They must be very fond of each other. I heard him murmuring her name last night in his sleep. He set me thinking of my own poor wife. What are they doing now, Crayford, in the old house in Devonshire?

CRAYFORD: (*Snow*) Not despairing yet, if my sister Lucy is still among them. She has the gift of hoping and making others hope, God Bless her!

(*A hail outside—" 'Sea Mew' ahoy." Frank wakes up, and the vision vanishes. Crayford and Steventon rise. The door is opened, and the men and officers of the "Wanderer" enter, headed by Capt. Helding and Richard Wardour. Richard Wardour has a gun with him. These two come down to the front and greet the officers of the "Sea Mew," Capt. Helding shaking hands cordially, Wardour nodding gruffly to Steventon and Frank, and only shaking hands with Crayford. The remainder of the "Wanderer's" men group themselves at the back.*)

CRAYFORD: (*Shaking hands with Capt. Helding*) Captain Helding, I am heartily glad to see you. Now my men, the cask in the middle, here. (*Goes up with the Captain.*)

WARDOUR: (*Standing between Steventon and Frank*) What are we wanted here for?

STEVENTON: To consult, I suspect, on the best means of escaping from this horrible place.

WARDOUR: *You* may think it horrible—*I* like it.

ALDERSLEY: Like it! Good Heavens! Why?

WARDOUR: (*Seating himself in a corner*) Because there are no women here.

(*Snow ceases gradually.*)

ALDERSLEY: (*Seating himself on a bench with Steventon*) Just as great a bear as ever!

CRAYFORD: (*Placing himself at the cask, with Captain Held-ing by his side and the dice-box before him*) Brother officers and men of the "Wanderer" and "Sea Mew"!—The Commander of this Expedition, Capt. Ebsworth, is, I grieve to say, too ill to rise from his bed and address you himself. He has therefore given me his directions, as his second in command, and I now have the honour of speaking to you in his place. Without recalling all the hardships we have suffered for the last three years—the loss first of one of our ships, then of the other, the deaths of some of our bravest and best companions, the vain battles we have been fighting with the ice and snow and boundless desolation of these inhospitable regions—without dwelling on these things, it is my duty to remind you that this, the last place in which we have taken refuge, is far beyond the track of any previous expedition, and that consequently our chance of being discovered by any rescuing parties that may be sent to look for us is, to say the least of it, a chance of the most uncertain kind. You all agree with me, Gentlemen, so far?

THE OFFICERS: (*With the exception of Wardour who re-mains silent throughout the scene*) Yes! Yes!

CRAYFORD: It is therefore urgently necessary that we should make another, and probably a last, effort to extricate ourselves. The winter is coming on, game is getting scarcer and scarcer, our stock of provisions is running low, and the sick—especially, I am sorry to hear, the sick in the "Wanderer's" hut—are increasing in number, day by day. We must look to our own lives, and to the lives of those who are dependent on us—and we have no time to lose.

THE OFFICERS: Right! Right!—no time to lose.

CRAYFORD: The plan proposed is that a detachment of the ablebodied officers and men among us should set forth this very day, and make another effort to reach the nearest fur settlements, from which help and provisions may be dispatched to those who remain here. The new direction to be taken and the various precautions to be adopted, are all drawn out ready, the only question now before us, is who is to stop here, and who is to undertake the journey?

THE OFFICERS: Volunteers!

THE MEN: Aye, Aye, volunteers.

CAPTAIN HELDING: (*At the same time*) Not volunteers. No, No.

CRAYFORD: Wardour, do you say nothing?

WARDOUR: Nothing. Go, or stay—it's all one to me.

CRAYFORD: I am sorry to hear it. (*To the rest*) Well, suppose we say volunteers—who volunteers—to stay?

(*Dead silence. The officers and men look at each other confusedly.*)

CRAYFORD: You see we can't settle it by volunteering. You all want to go. Every man among us, who has the use of his limbs, naturally wants to go. But what is to become of those who have *not* got the use of their limbs. Some of us must stay and take care of the sick.

THE OFFICERS: True! True!

CRAYFORD: So we get back again to the old question, who among the ablebodied is to go, and who is to stay? Capt. Ebsworth says, and I say, let chance decide it!

OFFICERS AND MEN: Hear! Hear! Hear! Hurrah!

CRAYFORD: Here are dice. The numbers run as high as twelve —double sixes. All who throw under six, stay, all who throw over six, go. Is that agreed?

THE OFFICERS: Agreed! Agreed!

CRAYFORD: The people shall decide by throwing lots into a hat, if they prefer it. Here (*taking a packet from his pocket*) are a certain number of folded pieces of paper. Half have "Stay" written inside, and half, "Go." Men of the "Wanderer" and "Sea Mew" both, which will you have the hat or the dice?

THE MEN: The Hat!

CRAYFORD: Very well. A hat there!

JOHN WANT: (*Comes forward from among the men with a saucepan*) What do you say to this, Sir?

CRAYFORD: Not a hat among us without a hole in it, I suppose. Well! We must put up with the saucepan, and the Cook shall hand it round. (*Turns papers into saucepan.*) Shake it well!

JOHN WANT: May I draw first, Sir?

CRAYFORD: The Cook ought to stay by the kitchen.

JOHN WANT: Not when he has nothing to put in his saucepan but paper, Sir. (*General laugh.*)

CRAYFORD: Well, well. I admit the plea. Draw, my men. The officers, in order of seniority, throw meanwhile. The Captain of the "Wanderer" throws first. Under six—"Stay." Over six—"Go." There is the box, Captain Helding. (*Hands the box to the Captain—speaks to one of the officers.*) Take the slate, and mark down those who go, and those who stay.

(*Men draw lots. Officers cast dice. Exclaim at intervals "Go!" and "Stay!"*)

CAPTAIN HELDING: (*Casting*) Seven!

CRAYFORD: "Go!" I congratulate you, Sir. Now for my own chance. (*Casts*) Three!—Stay!—Ah, well, well if I can do my duty and be of use to others what does it matter whether I go or stay? Wardour, you are next in the absence of your first lieutenant. (*Wardour prepares to cast without shaking the box.*) Shake the box, man! Give yourself a chance of luck!

WARDOUR: (*Letting the dice fall out carelessly*) Not I! I've done with luck. (*Goes back to his place without looking at the dice.*)

CRAYFORD: Six! There you have a second chance in spite of yourself. You are neither under nor over—you throw again.*

WARDOUR: Bah! It's not worth the trouble of getting up for. Somebody else throw for me. (*Looking at Frank*) You! You have got what the women call a lucky face.

ALDERSLEY: (*To Crayford*) Shall I?

CRAYFORD: Yes, if he wishes it.

ALDERSLEY: (*Casting*) Two!—He stays! Wardour, I am sorry I have thrown against you.

WARDOUR: I tell you again—go or stay, it's all one to me. You will be luckier when you cast for yourself.

CRAYFORD: It is his turn to throw for himself now.

ALDERSLEY: (*Casting*) Eight!—Hurrah! I go.

WARDOUR: What did I tell you? The chance was yours—you have thriven on my ill luck.

CRAYFORD: Steventon! It's your turn.

STEVENTON: (*Casting*) Five!

CRAYFORD: Stay! We must comfort each other. Men who stay, file into the Inner Hut.

(*They do so. Snow heavily. Music, "Spoilt Child" until Captain Helding goes out after his men.*) [5]

* (*Snow ready.*)

[5] This part of the MS has been revised and Dickens' prompt note is not clear. It reads (*Gives box to Charles Collins. Charles Collins, Marcus Stone and William Webster throw on the chest. Charles Collins throws to Go. Marcus Stone throws to Stay and W. Webster throws to Go. Among the men directly afterwards, Young Mark Lemon throws to Go and M. Luard throws to Go; also George Evans throws to Go.*). C. Collins was given Darker's role at Manchester. He, Stone, and Webster apparently played as unnamed officers in the earlier performances. Dickens changed the action and dialogue so the "men" could draw lots while the

CAPTAIN HELDING: Men who go, the Rendezvous is at this hut as soon as we can be ready for the journey. A couple of hands here, Lieutenant Crayford, to shovel away the drift—it chokes the door.

STEVENTON: (*Calling*) A couple of hands there with shovels to clear the snow from the door.

CRAYFORD: Here are the directions for the journey. (*Gives paper.*)

(*Exit Captain Helding accompanied by his officers. Bateson and Darker shut the door.*) [6]

ALDERSLEY: (*Going to his berth*) I shall pack at once. It won't take me two minutes. (*Rolls up his blankets, etc.*)

CRAYFORD: (*To Wardour who is about to go*) Wardour, you are one of those who stay. You will not be wanted yet at the Hut. Wait here a little. I wish to speak to you.

WARDOUR: Are you going to give me any more good advice?

CRAYFORD: Don't look at me in that sour way. I am only going to ask you a question.

ALDERSLEY: (*Rolling up bundle, etc.*) There! I am all ready

officers threw dice, and thus shortened this action. He did not change the note, however. Presumably, Steventon gave the dice to C. Collins, but this is not clear.

[6] In a prompt note Dickens listed two divisions for the cast: Stay and Go; Sea Mew and Wanderer. In both lists, some names were deleted and others added, probably at Manchester as all the "Evans" were deleted. In the following, the deleted name has been put in parentheses. First list— *Stay: Crayford, Wardour, Steventon, M. Stone, Bateson, John Want, John; Go: Capt. Helding, Frank, Charles Collins, (W. Webster), Langford, M. Lemon Jr., Luard, (George Evans), Wood, Darker.* Second list—*Sea Mew: Crayford, Aldersley, Steventon, Bateson, Darker, John Want, (George Evans), Wood, John, Johnson; Wanderer: Helding, Wardour, (Charles Collins), Wilson, Marcus Stone, (Tom Evans), Nathan, (James Berger), Mark Lemon Jr., Luard, (Buller), (William Webster), Langford.*

for the March. Stop! I have forgotten my Snow-Shoes. (*Going out.*)

CRAYFORD: *Frank, have you taken everything that belongs to you out of your berth?

ALDERSLEY: Yes.

CRAYFORD: We are almost as short of fuel as we are of provisions. Your berth, having no one to shelter now, will make good firing. If you see Bateson in the Storehouse, send him here with his axe.

ALDERSLEY: Very well. (*Exit by the door in flat.*)

CRAYFORD: Wardour, we are alone at last.

WARDOUR: Well!

CRAYFORD: You have both disappointed and surprised me today. Why did you say that it was all one to you whether you went or stayed? Why are you the only man among us, who seems indifferent whether we are rescued or not?

WARDOUR: Can a man always give a reason for what seems strange in his manner or his words?

CRAYFORD: He can try—when his friend asks him.

WARDOUR: That's true. Do you remember the first night at Sea, when we sailed from England in the Wanderer?

CRAYFORD: As well as if it was yesterday.

WARDOUR: A calm, still night. No clouds, no stars. Nothing in the sky but the broad Moon, and hardly a ripple to break the path of light she made in the quiet water. Mine was the Middle Watch that night. You came on deck, and found me alone.

CRAYFORD: And in tears.

WARDOUR: The last I shall ever shed.

CRAYFORD: Don't say that. There are times when a man is to be pitied indeed, if he can shed no tears.

WARDOUR: I should have quarreled with any other man who

* (*Clear the set for the berths, and see wood is ready for Wardour. See John Thompson standing by.*)

had surprised me at that moment. There was something, I suppose, in your voice when you asked my pardon for disturbing me, that softened my heart. I told you I had met with a disappointment which had broken me for life. There was no need to explain further. The only hopeless wretchedness in this world, is the wretchedness that women cause.

CRAYFORD: And the only unalloyed happiness, the happiness they bring.

WARDOUR: That may be your experience of them. Mine is different. All the devotion, the patience, the humility, the worship, that there is in Man, I laid at the feet of a Woman. She accepted the offering as Women do—accepted it easily, gracefully, unfeelingly—accepted it as a matter of course. I left England to win a high place in my profession, before I dared to win her. I braved danger and faced death. I staked my life in the Fever-Swamps of Africa, to gain the promotion that I only desired for her sake—and gained it. I came back, to give her all, and to ask nothing in return but to rest my weary heart in the sunshine of her smile. I came back, to win the woman whom I had wrought for, all my life—wrought for, longer than Jacob wrought for Rachel. And her own lips—the lips I had kissed at parting—told me that another man had robbed me of her. I spoke but few words when we parted that last time, and parted for ever. "The time may come," I told her, "when I shall forgive *you,* but the man who has robbed me of you shall rue the day when you and he first met."

CRAYFORD: Wardour! Wardour! I would rather see you in tears again, than hear you say that.

WARDOUR: The treachery had been kept secret. Nobody could tell me where to find him; nobody could tell me who he was. What did it matter? When I had lived out the first agony, I could rely on myself—I could be patient, and bide my time.

CRAYFORD: Your time! What time?

WARDOUR: The time when I and that man shall meet, face to face. I knew it then—I know it now—it was written on my heart then, it is written on my heart now, that we two shall meet, and know each other. With that conviction strong within me, I accepted this service, as I would have accepted anything that set work and hardship and danger, like Ramparts, between my misery and me. With that conviction strong within me still, I tell you it is no matter whether I stay here with the sick, or go hence with the strong—I shall live 'till I have met that man. There is a day of Reckoning appointed between us. Here, in the freezing cold, or away in the deadly heat—in battle or in ship-wreck—in the face of starvation or under the shadow of Pesti-lence—though hundreds are falling around me, I shall live! Live, for the coming of one day—live for the meeting with one man!

CRAYFORD: Wardour!

WARDOUR: (*Interrupting*) Look at me! Look how I have lived and thriven, with the heart-ache gnawing at me at home, with the winds of the Icy North whistling round me here! I am the strongest man among you. Why? I have fought through hard-ships that have laid the best-seasoned men of all our party on their backs. Why? What have I done that my life should throb as bravely through every vein of my body at this minute, and in this deadly place, as ever it did in the wholesome breezes of Home? What am I preserved for? I tell you again, for the coming of one day—for the meeting with one man.

CRAYFORD: Wardour, since we first met, I have believed in your better nature against all outward appearance. I have be-lieved in you, firmly, truly, as your brother might. You are putting that belief to a hard test. If your enemy had told me that you had ever talked as you talk now—that you had ever looked as you look now—I would have turned my back on him as the utterer of a vile calumny against a just, a brave, and upright,

Man. O my friend, my friend, if ever I have deserved well of you, put away those thoughts from your heart! Face me again, with the stainless look of a man who has trampled under his feet the bloody superstitions of revenge, and knows them no more! Never, never, let the time come when I cannot offer you my hand, as I offer it now, to the man I can still admire—to the brother I can still love!

WARDOUR: (Aside) Why did I speak? Why did I distress him? (To Crayford) You are kinder to me than I deserve. Be kinder still, and forget what I have said. No, no, no more talk about me; I am not worth it. We'll change the subject, and never go back to it again. Let's do something. Is there no work in hand? No game to shoot, nothing to cut, nothing to carry? Hard work, Crayford, that's the true Elixer of *our* life! Hard work that stretches the muscles and sets the blood a-glowing, that tires the body and rests the mind! (*Enter Bateson with an axe.*) Here's a man with an axe. I'll do his work for him, whatever it is. (*Snatches the axe from Bateson, and gives him the gun.*)

BATESON: (To Crayford) Captain Ebsworth wishes to see you, Sir.

CRAYFORD: (Looking at Wardour) Wardour, you won't leave the Hut till I come back?

WARDOUR: No! no!

(*Exit Crayford.*)

BATESON: (Holding out his hand for the axe, and offering the gun) I beg your pardon, Sir—

WARDOUR: Nonsense! Why should you beg my pardon? Give me your work to do. My arm is stiff, and my hands are cold. Go you and look for the Bear I have failed to find. Some other man always finds what I miss—What was this axe wanted for?

BATESON: (Pointing) To cut up Lieutenant Aldersley's Berth there, into firewood, Sir.

WARDOUR: I'll do it. I'll have it down in no time.

BATESON: (*Aside*) He looks as if he'd have the whole hut down in no time, if he only got the chance of chopping at it. (*Exit.*)

WARDOUR: *If I could only cut my thoughts out of me, as I am going to cut the billets out of this wood! (*Striking at the Berth*) Down it comes! A good axe! O me, if I had been born a Carpenter instead of a Gentleman!—Crash you go! Something like a grip on this handle!—Poor Crayford! His words stick in my throat—Crash again!—A fine fellow, a noble fellow!—Good again!—No use thinking, no use regretting,—What is said, is said.—Another plank out! It does not take much, Young Aldersley, to demolish *your* nest! Have at the back now. One, two, and down it comes. (*Tears out a long strip of wood.*) This must be cut in half.—Stop! What's here! A name carved in the wood! C.L.A.—Clara. (*Throwing down the wood*) Damn the fellow and his sweetheart too, why must she have that name, of all the names in the world!—The axe—where the Devil is the axe!— Work, work, work; nothing for it but work! (*Cuts out another plank.*) More carving! That's the way these young Idlers employ their long hours—F.A. These are his initials. Frank Aldersley— and under them here?—C.B.! His Sweetheart's Initials. Why, *her* cipher is C.B.—C.B.! Clara Burnham!—Nonsense!—Why Burnham, because the letter is B.? Hundreds of names—thousands—begin with B.—Where's the axe?—Crayford, come here, and let's go hunting. I don't like my own thoughts—I am cold, cold, all over. (*Goes to the fire and holds his hands over it.*) How they tremble! Steady, steady, steady! (*A pause. His voice drops to a whisper, and he looks all round him suspiciously.*) Has the day come, and the man? Here, at the end of the world? Here, at the last fight of all of us against starvation and death.†

* (*Carpenter to stand with pieces of wood behind Aldersley's berth.*)
† (*Snow ready.*)

(*Enter Crayford.*)

CRAYFORD: Did I hear you call me?—Good Heaven, Wardour, how pale you are? Has anything happened?

WARDOUR: (*Hastily folding a handkerchief round his left hand*) I hurt myself with the axe—it's nothing—never mind. Pain has always a curious effect on me. I tell you it's nothing—don't notice. Where's Aldersley? * He's a good fellow, isn't he? You know him well—the sort of fellow the women take to—likely to get on with them? God save you man, how you stare at me! Where's Aldersley?

ALDERSLEY: (*Entering*) Here! Who wants him? I wish he was in better marching order.

WARDOUR: (*Taking him abruptly by the arm*) Not strong, eh? You don't look it. I didn't speak civilly to you when you were casting the dice. I apologize. Shake hands. Come on! Not strong, eh? The dice had better have sent me away, and kept you here. I never felt in better condition in my life. We men of Kent are made of tough material.

ALDERSLEY: You come from Kent?

WARDOUR: From East Kent. Do you know that part of the country?

ALDERSLEY: (*Aside*) I ought to know something about East Kent, for some dear friends of mine once lived there.

WARDOUR: Ah? One of the County Families, I suppose? (*Suddenly to Crayford*) Why do you still stare at me so?

CRAYFORD: Why are you still looking unlike yourself?

WARDOUR: (*To Frank*) One of the County Families, of course. The Witherbys of Yew Grange, I dare say?

ALDERSLEY: No; but friends of the Witherbys, very likely—the Burnhams.

WARDOUR: (*Turning aside suddenly, lets the handkerchief*

* (*Snow for Frank's entrance.*)

drop from his hand, which he presses convulsively over his heart.) Quiet! Quiet!

CRAYFORD: (*Picking up the handkerchief, and offering it significantly to Wardour*) You have dropped your bandage. Strange—

WARDOUR: (*Fiercely*) What's strange?

CRAYFORD: That there should be no blood on it.

WARDOUR: (*Snatching it away*) Next time you see it, there may be a stain or two. (*To Frank*) So you know the Burnhams? What became of Clara when her Mother married again?

ALDERSLEY: (*Haughtily*) Clara! What authorizes you to speak of the young lady in that familiar way?

WARDOUR: What right have you to ask me?

ALDERSLEY: (*Aside*) Why should I mind mentioning it? (*To Wardour*) Right?

WARDOUR: Yes. Right?

ALDERSLEY: The right of being engaged to marry her.*

(*Wardour turning away again, his left hand slips down to a knife which he wears round his waist.*)

CRAYFORD: (*Standing on that side observes it*) You forget (*seizing his hand*) that your hand is hurt.

WARDOUR: (*To Frank, with over-strained politeness*) Impossible to dispute such a right as yours. Perhaps you will excuse me, when you know that I am one of Miss Burnham's oldest friends. My father and her father were neighbors. We always met like brother and sister.

ALDERSLEY: (*Warmly*) Say no more. I was in the wrong. Pray forgive me!

WARDOUR: Is she very fond of you?

ALDERSLEY: What a question! Make one at my wedding when we get back to England, and judge for yourself.†

---

* (*Snow ready.*)
† (*Snow heavily until end of Act.*)

WARDOUR: (*Aside*) Make one at your wedding? (*Knock at the door in flat. It opens and Captain Helding enters.*) Yes—if you can walk to it out of your grave!

(*Men of the exploring party appear outside. Music, "River, River" until Act Drop.*)

CAPTAIN HELDING: We are ready.

ALDERSLEY: And I am ready. I go! (*Throwing his snow-shoes over his shoulder.*)

WARDOUR: (*Aside*) And I stay? Stay when the day of Reckoning is come? Stay, when I have him at last?

CAPTAIN HELDING: (*To Crayford*) I have a casualty to report, which diminishes our numbers by one. (*Wardour starts, and listens anxiously.*) My second Lieutenant, who was to have joined the Exploring Party, has had a fall on the Ice, and, I fear, has broken his leg.

WARDOUR: I will supply his place.

CRAYFORD: (*Looking alternately at Wardour and Frank*) No! Not you.

WARDOUR: Why not?

CAPTAIN HELDING: Why not, indeed? Wardour is the very man to be useful on a long march. I was thinking of him myself. He is the healthiest of the party.*

CRAYFORD: He has no right to volunteer. We settled that chance should decide who was to go, and who was to stay.

WARDOUR: And chance *has* decided it. Do you think we are going to cast the Dice again, and give an Officer of the Sea Mew a chance of replacing an officer of the Wanderer? There is a vacancy in our party, not in yours. And we claim the right of filling it as we please. I volunteer and my Captain backs me. Whose authority is to keep me here, after that? (*Calling*) Give me my gun there!—Where is that man?—Give me my gun!

CAPTAIN HELDING: He is right, Crayford. The missing man

* (*Stand by Everybody. Snow very hard.*)

belongs to my Hut, and in common justice, one of my officers ought to supply his place.

(*Captain Helding takes leave of the officers. Exits to his men. John Want gives Go party bottles, etc. out of the box. The two parties of men take leave of each other. The Stay party gives three cheers. The Go party respond. Two men at the sledge.*)

CRAYFORD: No hope that way. (*Turns to Frank*) Frank, Frank!

ALDERSLEY: Yes. What is it?

CRAYFORD: Take the advice of an old friend who wishes you well.

WARDOUR: Let him alone! Let him alone!

CRAYFORD: Frank, don't risk hardships you are unfit to bear.

WARDOUR: Let him alone!

CRAYFORD: (*With great earnestness*) Frank, you feel, yourself, how weak illness has left you, and how unfit you are to brave the exposure to cold, and long marches over the snow.

WARDOUR: (*Suddenly taking Crayford by the throat*) What do you mean! Leave him to his choice.

(*Crayford catches Wardour's hand quietly in both of his. Frank interposes between them from behind. Crayford releasing one of his hands, puts Frank away with the other; all the time looking steadily in Wardour's face.*)

CRAYFORD: I said to you, Wardour, a little while ago, there are times when a man is to be pitied. I pity you, now. Take your hand away.

WARDOUR: (*Releasing him*) I beg your pardon.*

ALDERSLEY: Like a brave man! Come along!

WARDOUR: Bring me my gun there! (*Bateson brings it.*) Come then! Come over the Snow and the Ice! Come over the road that no human footsteps have ever trodden, and where no

* (*Act Drop ready.*)

human trace is ever left! (*Loads his gun, and rams the charge home.*)

ALDERSLEY: (*At the door*) God bless you, Crayford!

(*The men outside move off, leaving Frank alone in the snow.*)

CRAYFORD: (*Going to him, and seizing his hand*) Heaven preserve you, Frank! (*They shake hands, and Frank begins climbing the Drift.*) I would give all I have in the world to be with you. While you can stand, keep with the Main Body, Frank!

WARDOUR: While he can stand, he keeps with *Me!*

(*Exeunt Wardour and Frank. Crayford left alone in the Hut watching them over the snow.*)

CURTAIN

END OF THE SECOND ACT

THE FROZEN DEEP

Act the Third

Act III *

(Rises, Music, "Farewell to Lochabar" once. Scene: A Cavern on the Coast of Newfoundland, opening at the side, on another Cavern. In flat, opening on a bright view of Sea-Beach and Sea. On one side, John Want discovered, cording a box. On the other side, Nurse Esther, sitting on a fragment of rock, with her face hidden in her hands.)

JOHN WANT: *(Looking round at Nurse)* There's a nice kind of fellow-servant for a cheerful man like me to keep company with! That woman is one great heap of grumbling from head to foot. If I had known before I was rescued, that I was to have much of her society, I think I should have preferred staying at the North Pole. I was very happy, keeping up every body's spirits at the North Pole. I had a good deal of sleep at the North Pole. Taking one thing with another, I think I must have been very comfortable at the North Pole, if I had only known it. Another man in my place might be inclined to say that this Newfoundland Cavern was rather a sloppy, slimy, drafty, sea-weedy sort of a habitation to stop in. Another man might object to perpetual Newfoundland fogs, perpetual Newfoundland Cod Fish, and perpetual Newfoundland dogs. We had some very nice Bears at the North Pole. But never mind; it's all one to me; I don't grumble.

* *(Before ringing up, see Properties ready according to List. See that John Want has pipe and fire-box.)*

NURSE ESTHER: (*Looking up, irritably*) Man, man, ye do nought else.

JOHN WANT: Nothing else but grumble? Is this unjoyful old woman joking? *I* grumble! Whoever heard a word of complaint issue from my lips? Whoever saw a sour look on my face?

NURSE ESTHER: Face! D'ye ca' yon stickit thing o' th' top o' your shoulders, a face, (*aside*) but why do I waste words on him? He's just a puir weak creature!

JOHN WANT: (*Aside*) She's only a cracked old woman. Always a going on about her Second Sight! I don't believe her First Sight is much to boast of, far less mentioning a second one. Second Sight! (*With great contempt*) No woman but a Scotch woman would set any vally by a second hand eye. And, like other second hand articles, it's mostly made up of bits that she picked up here, and bits that she picked up there; and then she goes and pieces them together, sometimes right and oftener wrong, and then forgets she did it, being a Muddle-headed female, and sets up for a prophet. Besides, she's a going fast. She won't last out the voyage back to England. How many of us will? (*Nurse rises and goes to back.*) It's very damp here. I have heard a great deal of coughing about me, and some of the men look dreadful delicate. I shall be agreeably surprised if we all get back alive to England, I shall indeed.

(*Music, "Spoilt Child" once. Enter Bateson by opening in flat. Nurse Esther goes to the back of the Stage, and looks out on the sea view.*)

BATESON: Look sharp with your work there, John Want. The ladies will be coming in here, directly.

JOHN WANT: If they have any regard for their constitutions in general, and their lungs in particular, they will keep out.

BATESON: Will they? It's my opinion, they will do nothing of the sort. Mrs. Steventon and Miss Ebsworth are within two

minutes walk of the Cave, and Miss Crayford and Miss Burnham are not far behind them.

JOHN WANT: Bateson, I consider you to be as sharp a man as
myself—though not so cheerful. I want to know something
about these ladies. As yet I can't for the life of me make out how
they have got here on the coast of Newfoundland, can you?

BATESON: As I happen to have the use of my eyes and ears, I
should say I could. What is it you want to make out? You know,
as well as I do, that we were saved from starving and freezing to
death by a searching expedition from England, which discovered
us in that Arctic hut of ours. Well, the ladies are here—as I have
heard them say a dozen times already—because they followed
that expedition, to meet it on its return from the miserable
North Pole.

JOHN WANT: Don't grumble. I won't hear any grumbling.
Miserable North Pole, indeed! What do you call this place? But
never mind—

BATESON: Well, and the ship in which the ladies took passage
encountered the ship in which we sailed out of the Arctic Seas,
abreast of this coast of Newfoundland. And, as far as I can
understand it, we have all come ashore here for a day or two, for
the sake of the health of these same ladies, after the confinement
which they have undergone on board their vessel. That's all I
know about it, and that's all I mean to say; for (looks off) here
come two of the ladies, and Captain Ebsworth with them.

(Enter Lieutenant Steventon, Mrs. Steventon, Captain Ebsworth, and Rose. Bateson touches his hat, and goes out. Nurse
Esther comes down to front. John Want continues cording the
box.)

STEVENTON: (To Captain Ebsworth) There is some of the
baggage still to be stowed away in the boat, Captain Ebsworth.
Shall I go and give the men their orders?

CAPTAIN EBSWORTH: There is no need. I have a report to receive from one of the midshipmen, who is now awaiting me on the Beach; and I will give him the necessary directions. (*To his daughter*) Rose my love, wait here. I will come back for you.

ROSE: Don't be long, father. I have not seen half enough of you yet.

(*Captain Ebsworth takes leave of her, and exit.*)

MRS. STEVENTON: (*Pointing to Nurse*) Here is the poor old Nurse, just as gloomy as ever. Let us try, Rose, if we can't cheer her a little. (*Goes with Rose and talks with Esther.*)

STEVENTON: (*To John Want*) Have you done cording that box?

JOHN WANT: I have done it as well as I can, Sir, but the damp of this place is beginning to tell upon our very ropes—I say nothing about our lungs—I only say, our ropes.

STEVENTON: Pooh! To look at your wry face and hear your croaking voice, one would think that our rescue from the Arctic Regions, was a downright misfortune. You deserve to be sent back.

JOHN WANT: I could be just as cheerful as ever, Sir, if I was. I hope I am thankful, but I don't like to hear the North Pole run down, in such a sloppy place as this. It was very clean and snowy at the North Pole, and it's very damp and sandy here. Do you never miss your bone soup now, Sir? *I* do. It mightn't have been strong, but it was very hot, and the cold seemed to give it a kind of Meaty flavor as it went down. (*Steventon coughs.*) Was it you that was a coughing so long last night, Sir? I don't presume to say anything against the air of this place, but I should be glad to know it wasn't you that was a coughing so hollow. Would you be so obliging as just to feel the state of these ropes with the ends of your fingers, Sir? You can dry them afterwards on the back of my jacket.

STEVENTON: You ought to have a stick laid across the back of your jacket. Take that box down to the boat directly. A croaking vagabond! He would have grumbled in the Garden of Eden.

JOHN WANT: I could be cheerful anywhere, Sir—but there must have been a great deal of troublesome work with the Flower-Beds, in the Garden of Eden! (*Exit with the box.*)

NURSE ESTHER: (*To Mrs. Steventon and Rose*) Where's the use o' telling me to be comforted, when ye keep me and my Nurse-child, Clara, apart?

ROSE: Surely not apart, when you and Clara are both here with the rest of us, on the coast of Newfoundland.

NURSE ESTHER: I sailed fra' England i' the same ship wi' Clara, but was I in Clara's cabin? I am here i' th' same wild land wi' Clara, but do I sleep at her feet? Do I go out wi' Clara to the yellow sands? Am I bye when she looks ower sea yon, for the ship that shall never come? For the ship that shall ne'er bring back the plighted lover, lost beyond the Frozen Deep?

STEVENTON: Why do you separate them?

MRS. STEVENTON: Because Esther is superstitious herself, and makes her young mistress superstitious too. Now, when we know the dreadful truth that Frank Aldersley is among the missing men, hardly a word passes Nurse Esther's lips which it is not ruin to Clara to hear.

NURSE ESTHER: Said I a' false when I said they were lost? Came not the time when ye a' left the auld house—when ye could bide no longer—when ye took ship yer ain sel, and sailed awa' here to the strange land, to meet the Seekers on their return? To get for yer ain sel, the tidings ye had no patience to let others get for ye? I mind it weel. The ship was abreast o' this barren land when ye heard the cry o' "Sail!" Ye crowded on the deck, and me amang ye. The mist was flying off before the sun and the morning breeze; and a' alang the path o' light, and ower the leaping waves, the Ships o' the Seekers came booming down on us. The voices cheered fra' the decks. The bright flag flew up, like a Lark, into the morning sky. And ye a' fell on your knees and lookit up into the sunny Heavens, and wept.

(*Exeunt Mr. and Mrs. Steventon.*)

ROSE: O Nurse, Nurse, think of Clara! Think of Frank Aldersley! And say no more!

NURSE ESTHER: I said, lang syne, in England, that they were lost. Said I a' false? The Seekers gave you back your father, gave Lucy Crayford back her brother, gave back her husband to the young wife that was wi' you, the noo,—but did they give back Frank Aldersley to my Nurse-child? Where there no lost men left, that no Seekers could find? And was Frank no amang them?

(*Mrs. Steventon looks in at the entrance of the Cave.*)

MRS. STEVENTON: (*Whispering*) Rose, Rose!

ROSE: (*Running to her*) Yes.

MRS. STEVENTON: Get Nurse Esther out of the way. (*Music, "Farewell to Lochabar," once, changing into "Has sorrow thy young days shaded,"—twice.*) Clara is coming. (*Exit.*)

ROSE: Here! Nurse, Nurse! Come in here. (*Pointing to the side Cavern*) I want to speak to you.

NURSE ESTHER: What for in there? Is Clara there?

ROSE: Yes, yes. Come, come Nurse, come with me.

(*Exit, leading Esther with her into side cavern. Enter Clara by the opening in flat, with Lieutenant Crayford and Lucy, on either side, leading her.*)

LUCY: You feel stronger and better, Love, after your little walk in the fresh air?

CLARA: I am stronger, Lucy, than you think. The sunshine strengthens me. My heart feels warmer in it. You have not seen any tears in my eyes—have you?—since the morning? I think I could answer for myself all day, but for the sailing of the ship, so soon, which is to take us back to England. Our approaching departure weighs heavily and more heavily on my spirits. Our going away from this place seems like giving up the last hope of Frank.

LUCY: (*Turning aside*) O how she wrings my heart!

CLARA: (*To Crayford*) I *must* hope still. *You* don't think him lost past all hope, I am sure?

CRAYFORD: (*Uneasily*) My dear young lady, my own position was once so hopeless that I ought to be the last man in the world to admit a thought of despair.

CLARA: (*Thoughtfully*) I see so much of the Mercy and Goodness of the Great Creator all around me—such brightness and beauty to delight us in the Earth and Heaven—such a blessed ending to all the past anxiety and sorrow of Lucy, and Caroline, and Rose, that I cannot lose hope. The very waves looked joyful as we walked along the shore just now. The poor stunted bushes on the cliff rustled as happily in the sweet air as the tall Elm Trees in our English home. When I heard them, I thought of the Trees that Frank and I used to walk under. Shall I see those Trees again, when we get back to England—and not see Frank! Shall I never, never shew him the withered leaves of his Nosegay, which I have kept here so long, for his sake! O! I *must* hope, and you must help me by hoping too!

CRAYFORD: (*Turning away his head*) What *can* I say to her!

LUCY: You know, Love, that I have but one hope now. The hope that I shall yet see you happy.

CLARA: (*To Crayford*) Don't look distressed. (*Takes his hand.*) I seem to have known you all my life. I can't help treating you, almost as familiarly as Lucy does. She tells me you were always fond of Frank. You must often have taken his hand in kindness. It is such a real comfort to me now, to take yours. (*Kisses his hand.*)

CRAYFORD: My dear, dear child! Don't talk so. (*Dashes his*

hand across his eyes.) What has come to me? Am I going to set two women an example of crying?

CLARA: Yes, yes; let us talk of Frank. I like to hear how brave he was when he left the Hut, and went out with the best of them to battle his way through the Snow. Lucy, he was the youngest of all, but he was as steady and brave as the best Seaman of the crew. He slung his snow-shoes over his shoulder with a smile. There was not a trembling tone in his voice, when he said Good Bye for the last time. (*To Crayford*) You said that Nelson himself never faced danger more bravely than my Frank?

CRAYFORD: Never.

CLARA: And how gentle he always was, with me! (*Lays her head on Lucy's shoulder.*)

LUCY: My love, you are beginning to look pale again. You want rest. Come inside. You can rest nicely, inside.

CRAYFORD: (*Crossing to Lucy behind Clara, and whispering*) Are any of our Officers in there?

LUCY: How can any of our Officers be there? Did we not see them all employed on the Beach? Come, Clara; come in, and rest!

CLARA: Let me go alone, Lucy. I have kept you too much apart from your brother, already. Pray give me my way in this; pray let me go alone!

LUCY: You must promise then to call, the moment you want me.

CLARA: (*Kissing her*) Always thinking of others; never of yourself! (*To Crayford*) We hope for Frank. Remember, we all three still hope for Frank! (*Exit into the Inner Cavern.*)

CRAYFORD: Every look, every word, that escapes her, goes to my soul. Hope! If she knew the whole truth, she would never hope again.

LUCY: William, you seem strangely anxious to keep Clara and your brother Officers as much apart as possible. Where would be the harm, if she did happen to meet with any of them while we are here?

CRAYFORD: She might talk to them—

LUCY: Well?

CRAYFORD: And might hear—

LUCY: Well?

CRAYFORD: What might kill her on the spot.

LUCY: In Heaven's name, why do you say that?

CRAYFORD: Is she out of hearing?

LUCY: Far, far! Have you been deceiving her—have you been deceiving me? What is the truth? Frank is one of the missing men, who formed the Exploring Party. And Wardour is one of the men who remained in the Hut. He must have died there, before you were found and rescued, or you would have brought him back. I gathered that, from what you said.

CRAYFORD: Lucy, I have still to tell you the worst. I said, before Clara, remembering how you cautioned me privately, this morning, to be careful in what I said to her, that there was division in the councils of the Exploring Party after they had been three days out. I told you that one portion of the men returned to the Hut, and that the other portion pushed forward with Frank.

LUCY: You mentioned the names of the men who went on with Frank.

CRAYFORD: I was obliged to mention names, or Clara might have suspected something.

LUCY: But what names?

CRAYFORD: God forgive me the falsehood! I used the names of the Dead. Nor did I tell you—how could I, before Clara!—that Richard Wardour contrived to be one of the Exploring Party. Of all who served in our Ships, Frank Aldersley and Richard Wardour are the only missing men. (*Lucy clasps her hands in despair.*) It is hard, it is shameful, to say the thing that is false, but who could kill that sweet gentle creature with the dreadful truth? I trembled like a child in the darkness when the exploring party came back exhausted to the hut, and I heard who the two men were who had gone on without them. Of all the Forlorn Hope, poor Frank alone supported Wardour's fierce resolution to press on. The noble fellow believed that every forward footstep he took brought him nearer to his promised wife. The snow was falling fast, the view was narrowed over the icy wilderness, and Frank Aldersley and Richard Wardour were seen no more.

(*Clara appears at the inner cavern.*)

CLARA: (*Calling*) Lucy!

(*Crayford and Lucy both start.*)

LUCY: She hasn't heard you, William—she hasn't heard. (*To Clara*) Coming, my love. (*Exit.*)

CRAYFORD: (*Walking backward and forward in agitation*) If we were only in England, if we were only back at home, we might hope to keep the secret from her for the rest of her life. But here, surrounded by those who know the truth, there is a risk of her discovering the worst every hour in the day. (*Enter Bateson and Darker, bringing a small table and arranging meat, bread, etc. upon it.*) What is it? What do you want here?

BATESON: Dinner time, Sir. The officers and the ladies are just coming in from the beach. (*Assists Darker to spread the table.*)

(*Enter Lieut. Steventon, Mrs. Steventon, Capt. Ebsworth, Rose, and rescued officers, by opening in Flat.*)

STEVENTON: (*To Crayford*) We have finished with the water casks and the fish. It is within half an hour of flood tide and when the ship is ready to sail, she will fire a gun, hoist a flag and send a boat ashore.[7]

CRAYFORD: (*In a low tone*) I can trust myself before Clara now. (*Exit into inner cavern.*)

STEVENTON: Well, ladies and gentlemen, (*exit Darker*) this is our last dinner on the coast of Newfoundland. Give me leave to propose a toast at the first round of the bottle. To our first dinner on the shores of old England! (*Mrs. Steventon and Rose look towards opening in Flat, and set their glasses down with a cry of alarm.*) What's the matter?

(*Music, "River, River" once. All rise. Wardour appears at opening in Flat, looking in at the party. He is clothed in rags; his hair is tangled and grey; his looks and gestures are those of a man whose reason is shaken, and whose bodily powers are sinking from fatigue.*)

STEVENTON: What a strange figure! Who are you?

WARDOUR: A starving man.

ROSE: Pray give him some food!

WARDOUR: Throw me some bones from the table. Give me my share along with the dogs. (*Advances a few steps.*)

STEVENTON: Bateson, give him some bread and meat. (*Bateson obeys.*) Where do you come from?

WARDOUR: (*Pointing to the distant view*) From the sea.

STEVENTON: Shipwrecked, I suppose? I heard something of a strange boat having been thrown on the beach thirty or forty miles higher up the coast. When were you wrecked, my man?

[7] This dialogue was added after the fair copy was made. It suggests that at Manchester Dickens may have had to dispense with the back cloth for Act III, on which the "Queen's ship" was rather small, or have had to call attention to it by having a small flag raised. No reviewer or observer of the Tavistock House or the Gallery of Illustration performances mentioned a flag being hoisted or a boat coming ashore.

WARDOUR: When? (*Pauses and makes gestures indicating an effort to collect his ideas.*) When? (*Shakes his head.*) I can't get the wash of the sea out of my ears. I can't get the shining stars all night, and the burning sun all day out of my brain. When was I wrecked? When was I first adrift in the boat? When did I get the tiller in my hand, and fight against hunger and sleep? When did the gnawing here (*touching his breast*) and the burning here (*touching his head*) first begin? I can't tell ye'. I have lost all reckoning of it. I can't eat, I can't sleep, I can't get the wash of the sea out of my ears. What are you baiting me with questions for? Let me eat.

STEVENTON: (*To Captain Ebsworth*) The poor wretch is out of his mind. Bateson, make a little weak grog in one of those empty bottles and give it to him.

MRS. STEVENTON: See! he is eating no more. What is he going to do with his bread and meat?

(*Wardour looks fixedly at the food in his hand—glances round, smiles, and puts the bread and meat in an old bag slung over his shoulder. Bateson gives him the rum and water.*)

WARDOUR: (*Drinking from the bottle and then holding it up to the light*) May I keep what's left?

STEVENTON: To be sure you may!

WARDOUR: (*Again looks round—then puts the bottle in the bag*) Women among ye? Are they English? Are they young? Let me look closer at them. (*Mrs. Steventon and Rose shrink back.*) No! That's not *her* face! No! Not found yet!

MRS. STEVENTON: Do pray ask him something about the woman he is looking for.

STEVENTON: Who is it you want to find? Your wife? (*Wardour shakes his head.*) Who then? What is she like?

WARDOUR: (*Sorrowfully and gently*) Young, with a fair sad face, with kind tender eyes, with a soft clear voice. Young and loving and merciful. I keep her face in my mind, though I can keep nothing else. I must wander, wander, wander—restless, sleepless, homeless—till I find her! Over the ice and over the snow—tossing on the sea, tramping over the land—awake all night, awake all day—wander, wander, wander, till I find *her!*

(*Enter Crayford from the inner cavern.*)

CRAYFORD: Who is that?

STEVENTON: A poor mad—

CRAYFORD: Mad? (*Looks steadily at Wardour.*) Mad? (*Recoils.*) Steventon! Ebsworth! Am *I* in my right senses? My God! it *is!*—(*seizing him*) Richard Wardour! (*Music, "River, River" until Wardour gives Frank to Clara.*) Alive! Alive to answer for Frank!

(*All start. Faint cry from Clara in inner cavern.*)

WARDOUR: Let me go!

CRAYFORD: Why are you here alone? Where is Frank, you villain! Where is Frank?

WARDOUR: Villain? And where is Frank? Ah! I think I know your meaning. I think I dimly understand.

CRAYFORD: (*To them all*) Look at this conscience-stricken wretch! Confess, unhappy ruin of a man! Tell us how it was done.

CLARA: (*Appears at side entrance, restrained by Lucy.*) I will see for myself! I heard Richard's name—I heard Frank's name. (*Breaks away. Lucy hides her face in her hands. Crayford tries to restrain Clara.*) Let me by! let me by! (*Faces Wardour standing alone, and stops petrified at the sight.*)

WARDOUR: (*With a low cry of recognition*) Found! (*Turns instantly, and breaks his way out of the cavern. Lucy hurries to Clara's side.*)

CRAYFORD: Follow him! On your lives follow him! (*Exeunt several.*)

CLARA: Frank, Frank, Frank!

(*Murmur without. Wardour rushes in, breathless and staggering, bearing Frank in his arms. Cheering from the men outside. Great sensation.*)

WARDOUR: (*To Clara*) Saved, saved for *you!* (*Releases Frank. Clara falls on Frank's bosom. Wardour looks at them, and speaks again after a moment in a faint, altered voice.*) He's footsore and weary, Clara. But I have saved him—I have saved him for *you!* I may rest now—I may sleep at last—the task is done, the struggle is over.

CLARA: (*Referring to Frank*) His poor feet! This way! here, here!

(*Leads Frank, with the assistance of the rest, except Crayford, to a chest at the back of the cave, where all close round them.*)

ALDERSLEY: (*Making an opening*) Where is Wardour? Help *him!* Never mind *me!* Help Wardour.

CRAYFORD: (*Supporting him*) Wardour! dear Wardour! Old friend whom I have wronged, remember and forgive me!

WARDOUR: (*Regardless of him*) I have made *her* happy. I may lay down my weary head now on the mother earth that hushes all her children to rest at last! Sink, heart! Sink, sink to rest! Look at them! They have forgotten *me* already.

CRAYFORD: Wardour, look at me! Look at your old friend!

WARDOUR: (*Vacantly*) My friend? Yes, yes, yes—he looks kindly at me—he looks like a friend. My eyes are dim, friend— my mind is dull—I have lost all memories but the memory of *her.* Dead thoughts—all dead thoughts but that one! And yet, he looks kindly? Why has his face gone down with the wreck of all the rest?—Hark ye, friend? Never let Frank know it! There was a time when the fiend within me hungered for his life.

CRAYFORD: Hush! hush!

WARDOUR: I took him away alone—away with me over the

waste of snow—he on one side, and the tempter on the other, and I between them, marching, marching, till the night fell and the camp-fire was all aflame. If you can't kill him, leave him when he sleeps—the tempter whispered me—leave him when he sleeps! I set him his place to sleep in apart; but he crept between the Devil and me, and nestled his head on *my* breast, and slept *here*. Leave him! Leave him!—the voice whispered— Lay him down in the snow and leave him! Love him—the lad's voice answered, moaning and murmuring *here,* in his sleep— Love him, Clara, for helping me! love him for my sake!—I heard the night-wind come up in the silence from the great Deep. It bore past me the groaning of the ice-bergs at sea, floating, floating past!—and the wicked voice floated away with it—away, away, away for ever! Love him, love him, Clara, for helping *me!* No wind could float that away! Love him, Clara,—(*His voice dies away and his head sinks.*)

ALDERSLEY: Help me up! I *must* go to him! Clara, come with me. (*Advances between Clara and Steventon.*) Wardour! Oh help Wardour! Clara, speak to him!

CLARA: Richard! (*No answer.*)

ALDERSLEY: Richard!

WARDOUR: Ah, poor Frank! I didn't forget you, Frank, when I came here to beg. I remembered you, lying down outside in the shadow of the rocks. I saved you your share of food and drink. Too weak to get at it now! A little rest, Frank! I shall soon be strong enough to carry you down to the ship!

ALDERSLEY: Get something to strengthen him, for God's sake! Oh, men! men! I should never have been here but for him! He has given all his strength to my weakness; and now, see how strong *I* am, and how weak *he* is! Clara! I held by his arm all over the ice and snow. *His* hand dragged me from the drowning men when we were wrecked. He kept watch when I was senseless in the open boat. Speak to him, Clara,—speak to him again!

CLARA: Richard, dear Richard, look at your old playmate! Have you forgotten me?

(*Music "River, River," merging at "kiss me before I die!" into "Those Evening Bells" which lasts until the Curtain has fallen.*)

WARDOUR: Forgotten you? (*Lays his hand on Frank's head.*) —Should I have been strong enough to save him, if I could have forgotten you? Stay! Some one was here and spoke to me just now. Ah! Crayford! I recollect now. (*Embracing him*) Dear Crayford! Come nearer! My mind clears, but my eyes grow dim. You will remember me kindly for Frank's sake? Poor Frank! Why does he hide his face? Is he crying? Nearer, Clara—I want to look my last at *you*. My sister, Clara!—Kiss me, sister, kiss me before I die!

(*Gun is fired from ship and boat is drawn to shore.*) [8]

[8] This is an addition to the fair copy. The boat is not mentioned in the reviews of the Tavistock House or Gallery of Illustration performances. It was probably added to the spectacle at Manchester.

CURTAIN

Bibliography

Works by Charles Dickens

Dickens, Charles. *Collected Papers.* 2 vols. Bloomsbury, 1937.

——. *The Letters of Charles Dickens.* Ed. Georgina Hogarth and Mamie Dickens. New York, n.d.

——. *Letters of Charles Dickens to Wilkie Collins.* Ed. Laurence Hutton. New York, 1892.

——. *Charles Dickens as Editor: Being Letters Written by Him to William Henry Wills His Sub-Editor.* Ed. R. C. Lehman. London, 1912.

——. *Mr. and Mrs. Charles Dickens: His Letters to Her.* Ed. Kate Perugini and Walter Dexter. London, 1935.

——. *The Love Romance of Charles Dickens: Told in His Letters to Maria Beadnell (Mrs. Winter).* Ed. Walter Dexter. London, 1936.

——. *The Letters of Charles Dickens.* Ed. Walter Dexter. 3 vols. Bloomsbury, 1938.

——. *The Heart of Charles Dickens: As Revealed in his Letters to Angela Burdett-Coutts.* Ed. Edgar Johnson. New York, 1952.

——. *The Poems and Verses of Charles Dickens.* Ed. F. G. Kitton. London, 1903.

——. *The Speeches of Charles Dickens.* Ed. K. J. Fielding. Oxford, 1960.

——. *The Dickens Theatrical Reader.* Ed. Edgar and Eleanor Johnson. Boston, 1964.

——. *Charles Dickens Rare Print Collection.* Ed. Seymour Eaton. Published for private circulation. Philadelphia, 1900.

——. "The Lost Arctic Voyagers," *Household Words,* X (1854), 361–365, 385–393, 433–437.

——. "Dr. Rae's Report," *Household Words,* X (1854), 457–459.

——. "Sir John Franklin and His Crews," *Household Words,* XI (1855), 12–20.

—— and Wilkie Collins. "The Lazy Tour of Two Idle Apprentices," *Household Words,* XVI (1857), 313–319, 337–349, 361–367, 385–393, 409–416.

Reviews of "The Frozen Deep"

"Tavistock-House Theatre," *The Times,* (London), January 7, 1857, p. 7.

"Music and the Drama," *The Athenaeum,* January 10, 1857, p. 56.

"Town and Table Talk on Literature, Art, Etc.," *The Illustrated London News,* January 10, 1857, p. 11.

"Mr. Wilkie Collins's 'The Frozen Deep,'" *The Leader: A Political and Literary Review,* January 10, 1857, pp. 44–45.

"The Theatres," *The Spectator*, January 10, 1857, p. 38.

"Tavistock House Theatricals," *The Examiner*, January 17, 1857, pp. 38–39.

"Tavistock House Theatricals," *The Illustrated London News*, January 17, 1857, pp. 51–52.

"In Remembrance of the Late Mr. Douglas Jerrold. Remaining Performances," *The Leader: A Political and Literary Review*, July 4, 1857, p. 632.

"Notes of the Week," *The Illustrated London News*, July 11, 1857, p. 35.

"The Late Mr. Douglas Jerrold," *The Times* (London), July 13, 1857, p. 12.

"Music and the Drama," *The Athenaeum*, July 18, 1857, p. 916.

"Town and Table Talk on Literature, Art, Etc.," *The Illustrated London News*, July 18, 1857, p. 59.

"The Jerrold Performances," *The Leader: A Political and Literary Review*, July 18, 1857, p. 692.

"Theatres and Music," *The Spectator*, July 18, 1857, p. 751.

"The Theatricals at the Gallery of Illustration," *The Saturday Review*, August 1, 1857, pp. 106–107.

"Olympic Theatre," *The Times* (London), October 29, 1866, p. 10.

"Music and the Drama," *The Athenaeum*, November 3, 1866, p. 576.

"The Theatres," *The Illustrated London News,* November 3, 1866, p. 438.

"The Theatrical Examiner," *The Examiner,* November 10, 1866, p. 711.

"The Frozen Deep," *The Dickensian,* XXX (1934), 118. (Report of a November 30, 1933, performance at Millicent Fawcett Hall Theatre in aid of the Funds of the Dickens House. The actors thought that they were re-enacting the 1857 performance, but, as made clear by a reference to the "clairvoyant heroine, Clara," they were using the 1866 version.)

Addenda

Report of the July 1855 performance of Collins' "The Lighthouse," reproductions of Stanfield's scenes of the lighthouse and of a ship in a storm, reprint of a woodcut, and an article from *The Illustrated London News. The Dickensian,* V (1909), 89, 91–94.

Facsimile playbill and brief comment on the Campden House production of "The Lighthouse" on July 10, 1855. *The Dickensian,* XXXVI (1940), 193–194.

Description of the typical performance at the Gallery of Illustration by Mr. and Mrs. Thomas German Reed, entertainers temporarily replaced by Dickens' cast. "Gallery of Illustration," *The Times* (London), December 16, 1856, p. 5.

Description of miscellaneous performances at the Gallery of Illustration by Brewer, Cavalier Poletti, and the Reeds. Cecil Howard and Clement Scott, *The Life and Reminiscences of E. L. Blanchard.* London, 1891, pp. 212, 223, 227, 260, 345.

Photograph of the Tavistock House schoolroom. *The Dickensian,* XXII (1926), 49.

Photograph of the amateur cast of "The Frozen Deep." *The Dickensian*, XXXVII (1940), 6.

Reproductions of two sketches made by Nathaniel Powers of scenes from the Tavistock House performances. *The Dickensian*, LVI (1960), 158.

Reprint of an *Illustrated London News* engraving that depicts the final scene of the Tavistock House performance. *The Dickensian*, XXXVI (1940), 194.

The false rumors about the Royal performance and the contemporary rebuttal. "Our Weekly Gossip," *The Athenaeum*, July 4, 1857, p. 854. "The Queen and Amateur Actors," *The Weekly Chronicle and Register*, July 4, 1857, p. 3.

List of the Queen's guests and attendants at the Royal performance. *The Times* (London), July 6, 1857, p. 8. *The Leader: A Political and Literary Review*, July 11, 1857, p. 658.

Detailed description of the Free Trade Hall, giving dimensions of the Grand Hall as 134 feet long, 78 feet wide, and 52 feet high. "Free Trade Hall, Manchester," *The Times* (London), October 8, 1856, p. 5.

A three-column report of the opening ceremonies giving history of the Anti-Corn League and of its role in raising money for the building. The chairman of the opening night on October 8 expressed hope that the Hall would help draw such men as Dickens to Manchester. "Free Trade Hall," *The Times* (London), October 10, 1856, p. 10.

Reproduction of a watercolor drawing showing part of the Manchester theater and of the stage. *The Dickensian*, LIV (1958), 130.

The public reports on the success of the Jerrold benefits signed by Dickens and Arthur Smith. "Miscellaneous News," *The Examiner*, September 5, 1857, p. 572. "The Arts," *The Leader*, September 5, 1857, p. 860.

Playbills. These were two-page circulars giving details such as the names of the cast, the price of the tickets (for the public performances), and the time of opening. The Pierpont Morgan MS collection M.A. 81 contains original bills for July 11 and 18 and for August 21 and 22. The *Charles Dickens Rare Print Collection*, ed. Seymour Eaton (published for private circulation; Philadelphia, 1900), contains several original bills, including ones for the January performances. The playbill for the August 24 performance is reproduced in *The Dickensian*, LIV (1958), 164.

One of several advertisements indicating that the 1866 version had an "improved" script. *The Times* (London), October 27, 1866, p. 8.

The Rae Controversy

Dr. John Rae's original report, written July 29, 1854, accompanied by an explanatory letter. *The Times* (London), October 23, 1854, p. 7.

Editorial raising question about the disturbing consequences of the report and about the credibility of the Eskimo witnesses. *The Times* (London), October 26, 1854, p. 6.

Letter from Captain T. B. Collinson accepting the report and proposing a plan to relieve the men on *H. M. S. Enterprise* still searching for Franklin. *The Times* (London), October 27, 1854, p. 8.

Reprint of Rae's July 29 report, engravings of Dr. Rae and of relics that he had purchased from the Eskimos, a list of twenty series of engravings that had been printed previously about the Franklin expedition and searches for its survivors. *The Illustrated London News*, October 28, 1854, p. 421.

Letter from E. J. H. [Rev. Edward J. Hornby] apologizing for an attack that he had made on Dr. Rae. *The Times* (London), November 3, 1854, p. 7.

Letter from Dr. Rae explaining why the dead sailors would have been grouped together when the Eskimos found them and why Franklin could not still be alive. *The Times* (London), November 7, 1854, p. 8.

The full government report. *Further Papers Relative to the Recent Arctic Expeditions in Search of Sir John Franklin and the Crews of H. M. S. "Erebus" and "Terror."* London, 1855. In particular, see "Proceedings of Dr. Rae," pp. 831–859.

[Henry Morley.] "The Lost English Sailors," *Household Words*, XV (1857), 145–147.

——. "Official Patriotism," *Household Words*, XV (1857), 385–390.

Report of Dickens' appearance as the public representative of periodical literature and the press which supported the Franklin rescue expedition. *The Times* (London), May 12, 1857, p. 12.

Report of the unveiling of Noble's statue of Sir John Franklin near Waterloo Palace, giving contemporary view of Franklin as a hero. *The Spectator*, November 17, 1866, p. 1271.

Selected Sources

Adrian, Arthur A. "A Note on the Dickens-Collins Friendship," *The Huntington Library Quarterly*, XVI (1952–53), 211–213.

[Ainger, Alfred.] "Mr Dickens's Amateur Theatricals: A Reminiscence," *Macmillan's Magazine*, XXIII (1870–71), 206–215.

Andersen, Hans Christian. *The Mermaid Man: The Autobiography of Hans Christian Andersen*. Trans. Maurice Michael. New York, 1955.

Ashley, Robert P. "The Career of Wilkie Collins." Unpublished dissertation, Harvard University, 1948.

——. *Wilkie Collins*. London, 1952.

——. "Wilkie Collins and the Dickensians," *The Dickensian*, XLIX (1953), 59–65.

——. "Wilkie Collins Reconsidered," *Nineteenth-Century Fiction*, IV (1949–50), 265–273.

Berger, Francesco. Letter about "The Frozen Deep" to the Editor, June 2, 1914. *The Dickensian*, X (1914), 193–194.

——. *97*. London, 1931.

Booth, Bradford A. "Wilkie Collins and the Art of Fiction," *Nineteenth-Century Fiction*, VI (1951–52), 131–143.

Bredsdorff, Elias. *Hans Andersen and Charles Dickens: A Friendship and its Dissolution*. Copenhagen, 1956.

Brown, T. J. "English Literary Autographs XV: Charles Dickens, 1812–1870," *The Book Collector*, IV, No. 3 (1955), 237. (An analysis of Dickens' handwriting.)

Browne, Edgar. *Phiz and Dickens*. New York, 1914.

Butt, John, and Kathleen Tillotson. *Dickens at Work*. London, 1957.

Clarke, Charles, and Mary Cowden. *Recollections of Writers.* London, 1878.

Collins, Wilkie. "The Lighthouse: A Drama in Two Acts." Not published; incomplete MS owned by the Berg Collection of the New York Public Library.

——. "The Frozen Deep: A Drama in Three Acts." Not published; printed by C. Whiting. London, 1866.

——. "The Frozen Deep: A Dramatic Story in Five Scenes," *Temple Bar,* XLII (1874), 1–21, 145–164, 289–316.

——. *The Frozen Deep and Other Stories.* 2 vols. London, 1874.

——. Letter to Mr. Kent, February 3, 1881. *The Dickensian,* V (1909), 161.

——. "The Use of Gas in Theatres," *The Mask: A Journal of the Art of the Theatre,* X (1924), 163–167. (Reprint of an article written in 1881.)

Cross, A. E. Brookes. "The Fascination of the Footlights," *The Dickensian,* XXIII (1927), 85–91. (Summary of Dickens' association with the theater.)

——. "The Influence of Dickens on the Contemporary Stage," *The Dickensian,* XXXIV (1937–38), 55–62. (Cross erroneously reports that the "prompt book" of the 1857 play is owned by the British Museum. It owns a copy of the 1866 printed text; Cross bases all his comments on this text, being unaware of the 1857 script.)

Davis, Neuel Pharr. *The Life of Wilkie Collins.* Urbana, Ill., 1956.

Dexter, Walter. "For One Night Only: Dickens's Appearances as an Amateur Actor," *The Dickensian*, XXXV (1939), 231–242; XXXVI (1939–40), 20–30, 91–102, 131–135, 195–201; XXXVII (1940), 7–11.

Dickens, Charles, Jr. "Reminiscences of My Father," *The Windsor Magazine*, LXXXI (December 1934), supplement.

Dickens, Henry Fielding. *Memories of My Father*. New York, 1929.

———. *The Recollections of Sir Henry Dickens, K. C*. London, 1934.

Dickens, Mary. *Charles Dickens*. London, 1885.

Eliot, T. S. *Selected Essays, 1917–1932*. New York, 1932.

Ellis, Stewart M. *Wilkie Collins, Sheridan Le Fanu, and Others*. London, 1931.

Engel, Monroe. "Dickens on Art," *Modern Philology*, LIII (1955–56), 25–38.

Fawcett, F. Dubrey. *Dickens the Dramatist*. London, 1952.

Fielding, Kenneth J. *Charles Dickens: A Critical Introduction*. London, 1958.

———. "Dickens and Wilkie Collins: A Reply," *The Dickensian*, XLIX (1953), 130–136.

Fields, James T. *Yesterday with Authors*. Boston, 1900.

Finch, Ernest Bliss. "The Mid-Victorian Theatre as Seen by Its Critics 1850–1870." Unpublished dissertation, Cornell University, 1951.

Fitz-Gerald, S. J. Adair. *Dickens and the Drama*. London, 1910.

Ford, George H. *Dickens and His Readers*. Princeton, 1955.

——. "Dickens's Notebook and 'Edwin Drood,' " *Nineteenth-Century Fiction*, VI (1952), 275–280.

Forster, John. *The Life of Charles Dickens*. Ed. J. W. T. Ley. London, 1928.

Franklin, John. *Narrative of a Journey to the Shores of the Polar Sea, in the Years 1819, 20, 21, and 22*. London, 1823.

Garis, Robert. *The Dickens Theatre*. London, 1965.

Gissing, George. *Charles Dickens: A Critical Study*. London, 1898.

——. *Critical Studies of the Works of Charles Dickens*. New York, 1924.

Grubb, Gerald G. "The Editorial Policies of Charles Dickens," *PMLA*, LVIII (1943), 110–124.

Hill, T. W. "The Enigma of Wilkie Collins," *The Dickensian*, XLVIII (1952), 54–57.

——. "The Late Wilkie Collins," *The Dickensian*, XLVIII (1952), 114–116.

House, Humphry. *The Dickens World*. London, 1961.

Howe, M. A. De Wolfe. *Memories of a Hostess: A Chronicle of Eminent Friendships Drawn Chiefly from the Diaries of Mrs. James T. Fields*. London, 1923.

Johnson, Edgar. *Charles Dickens: His Tragedy and Triumph.* 2 vols. New York, 1952.

Lehman, Rudolph C. *Memories of Half a Century: A Record of Friendships.* London, 1908.

Ley, J. W. T. *The Dickens Circle: A Narrative of the Novelist's Friendships.* London, 1918.

——. "Wilkie Collins's Influence Upon Dickens," *The Dickensian,* XX (1924), 65–69.

Macready, William Charles. *Macready's Reminiscences and Selections from His Diaries and Letters.* Ed. Sir Frederick Pollock. London, 1875.

Milley, Henry James Wye. "The Achievement of Wilkie Collins and his Influence on Dickens and Trollope." Unpublished dissertation, Yale University, 1941.

——. "Wilkie Collins and 'A Tale of Two Cities,'" *Modern Language Review,* XXXIV (1939), 525–534.

Morley, John. *Journal of a London Playgoer.* London, 1891.

Nelson, Harland S. "'Dickens' Plots: 'The Ways of Providence' or the Influence of Collins," *The Victorian Newsletter,* no. 19 (Spring 1961), 11–14.

Nicoll, Allardyce. *The English Theatre: A Short History.* London, 1936.

——. *A History of English Drama 1660–1900.* 6 vols. Cambridge, Eng., 1959.

Nisbet, Ada B. *Dickens and Ellen Ternan*. Berkeley, 1952.

Orwell, George. *Dickens, Dali, and Others: Studies in Popular Culture*. New York, 1946.

Phillips, Walter C. *Dickens, Reade, and Collins: Sensation Novelists, A Study in the Conditions and Theories of Novel Writing in Victorian England*. New York, 1919.

Richardson, Sir John. *Arctic Searching Expedition: A Journal of a Boat-Voyage Through Rupert's Land and the Arctic Sea*. London, 1851.

Robinson, Kenneth. *Wilkie Collins: A Biography*. London, 1951.

Ross, Sir John. *Narrative of a Second Voyage in Search of a Northwest Passage, and of a Residence in the Arctic Regions During the Years 1829, 1830, 1831, 1832, 1833*. London, 1835.

Stone, Marcus, R. A. "Some Recollections of Dickens," *The Dickensian*, VI (1910), 61–64.

Trilling, Lionel. "Introduction," *Little Dorrit*. London, 1953.

Van Loon, Hendrik. *Van Loon's Lives*. New York, 1942.

Wilson, Edmund. *Eight Essays*. Garden City, New York, 1954.

Wright, Thomas. *The Life of Charles Dickens*. London, 1935.

Zabel, Morton Dauwen. *Craft and Character: Texts, Method, and Vocation in Modern Fiction*. New York, 1957.